Sharon beautifully lays out a simple method of Bible study that will keep you coming back for more. Once you learn this way of reading God's Word, you will not just know about the Bible, but you will actually become intimately acquainted with the author, your Heavenly Father. As you spend time with Him, you will progressively become more joyful, peaceful, and hopeful. You will trust the one you know.

Fern Nichols, Founder, Moms in Prayer International,
and author, including of Silver Medallion Award winner,
Moms in Prayer: Standing in the Gap for Your Children

In *Give Me Wings to Soar*, Sharon's personality splashes onto every page, and readers feel like they're sitting with an encouraging friend gently pointing them to Christ. Using vivid examples from her own life, Sharon breaks down powerful biblical truths into digestible sizes so we can chew on them throughout the day. The only downside of the book is that it's hard to read only one devotional per day!

Cyndie Claypool de Neve, author of *God-Confident Kids* and coauthor of
Unshaken, Raise Them Up, and the devotional, *Start With Praise*

In her beautiful way of honest writing and reflecting, Sharon takes us by the hand and journeys with us directly to the heart of God. I feel like I know Him better by going through *Give Me Wings to Soar*, and it makes me hunger and thirst for a deeper intimacy with my Lord.

Nancy Lindgren, Founder and President, MORE Mentoring

I don't like to just 'read' a book, I prefer to 'work through' a book. So, author Sharon Gamble's new book, *Give Me Wings to Soar*, offers a perfect opportunity for both creativity and challenge. With a thematic and artistic thread of birds, this beautiful volume takes readers through learning how to establish a personal prayer rhythm, study the Bible, and incorporate God's truth into our daily lives. Each section: Nest (devotions), Flight (study), and Soar (journaling) serves to help us interact with all the fine teaching Gamble provides. I highly recommend this as a gift for anyone seeking to grow deeper in faith.

Lucinda Secrest McDowell, author of *Soul Strong* and *Life-Giving Choices*

Studying the Bible can be a daunting task for beginners. Where do you start? How do I study this giant book? How am I going to know what the lesson is? With Sharon's 4R Method, I have found my road map. The 4R Method has helped to show this new "study-er" of the Bible a way to spend time and take in what is written on the pages. I have sat in church listening to other people teach for years, but now I have the confidence to spend time each day learning what is in the depths of His teachings. Enjoy your time here and welcome to the Nest!

Maggie Rogers, Job and Life Skills Coach, and member of *Give Me Wings to Soar* test group

Sharon Gamble's book, *Give Me Wings to Soar*, leads you into intimate devotional times. I love how the author candidly shares personal struggles and then ties in the practical application of Scripture. She guides you to respond through targeted questions and calls to action based on the chosen verses. You will discover who you are as you follow her guidance, meditate on the truths found in the Word of God, pray, and journal your own discoveries. Get ready to soar!

Karen Sebastian Wirth, Hope Catalyst, speaker, and author of *The Power of Hope* series (*Prodigals, Mourning, Caregivers*)

Sharon Gamble has written a "must use" tool to help anyone wanting to study God's Word with intention and purpose. Whether you're young in your faith or more seasoned in studying God's Word, Sharon's quiet time format is simple and ignites a desire to look deeper into the words God is saying personally to you. It has rekindled a passion in my own quiet time as I am learning and seeing new insights based on the 4R Method. This is a fantastic resource and addition for studying God's Word.

Bonnie Nichols, Certified Life Coach and Founder, Wholehearted

As a woman who is made like Martha—a task-oriented mama of lively children—it can be challenging to get quiet before the Lord. Through the pages of *Give Me Wings to Soar*, Sharon invites your soul to take a seat as you receive God's love for you. Discover how to connect with God daily and be refreshed by Him through Sharon's encouragement and proven quiet time method.

Katie M. Reid, author of *Made Like Martha* and *A Very Bavarian Christmas*

Give Me Wings to Soar

A Sweet Selah Journey Toward a Deeper Walk with God

Sharon Gamble

Harris House Publishing

Give Me Wings to Soar: A Sweet Selah Journey Toward a Deeper Walk with God
Copyright 2020 by Sharon Gamble

Published by Harris House Publishing
harrishousepublishing.com
Colleyville, Texas
USA

Edited by Jan Peck
Cover and interior pages designed by Kathryn Bailey

ISBN: 978-1-946369-52-9 (pbk.)

Subject Heading: BIBLE STUDIES / WOMEN / CHRISTIAN LIFE

Dedicated

to my Wednesday Girls

Gratitude

Thank you to all the beautiful Wednesday Girls (over 200 of you!) who have attended Portsmouth Christian Academy's before-school Wednesday Girls group, sharing muffins and juice and studying the Word of God early in the mornings. Hearing your stories, praying for your hurts, and watching you grow into the fine women of God you are today has been among my greatest joys. This book is for you.

Thank you, Nest Bible study participants, for walking with me through the first draft of this book and faithfully doing the work each day. Oh, we did have fun together sharing "our verses" each week! Amanda, Anne, Eileen, Ellen, Janice, Jenn, Maggie, and Sue— you inspired me to keep writing, and you helped make the book better. I'm grateful for your enthusiasm and insights.

Thank you, Writers Club! Marlene, Jenn, and Amanda, you have prayed me through this past year, reading samples, offering suggestions, and always encouraging me to write for His glory. I love doing writing with you.

Thank you, Andi Cumbo-Floyd and all the gang at AndiLit. Coming from diverse backgrounds, you have encouraged me in devotional writing and taught me much about the process of writing a book. I appreciate each one of you.

Thank you, Sweet Selah team, board, and prayer team. You are the backbone in all I do, including writing this book. Your support and encouragement and especially your fervent

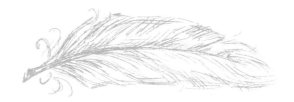

prayers have blessed me abundantly. Thank you to my parents, Ray and Margaret Fowler, for being constant cheerleaders and advisors as well as prayer warriors as I write. I am blessed beyond measure to be your daughter. Keep praying, please, that God uses this book for His glory and to draw His people closer to Himself.

Thank you, Jan, Terry, Kathryn, and my brother Ray, for your active work on this book. Jan, I am always astounded by the care you take with my words. You refine them, you analyze them, and you make sure they are true and right and best. I can't imagine a finer editor. I am forever grateful. Terry, you chose me as one of your authors when I was as yet unpublished and have helped me with a diligence and a selflessness that is amazing to behold. It's an honor to be a Harris House author. Thank you, Kathryn. You have done it again. Your design has captured the heart of what I'm seeking to share in this book. Thank you for the beautiful cover and the airy feathers and all that makes this book stand out as a write-worthy journal as well as a devotional study. You make my work look pretty, and I am grateful. Ray, the hours you spend taking a book full of designs and creating an e-book are legion. Thank you so very much for investing in my books this way. You make them a pleasure to read digitally. I am humbled by all four of you and your willingness to help and strive for excellence in this endeavor. May God bless you above and beyond!

Thank you to Ray and Mary as well. You two have prayed for me and encouraged me since I began this writing journey. I love my family, and I hope and pray that this book will one day be read by the next generation. This Nina can't sew patchwork quilts or create pretty artwork, but she can leave this legacy for those to come. May all my dear grands and those who come after them know that their Nina loved spending time with God and has prayed that each of them would find that nest of rest with Him each morning all the days of their lives.

To God Alone be the Glory
Soli Deo Gloria.
September 2020

CONTENTS

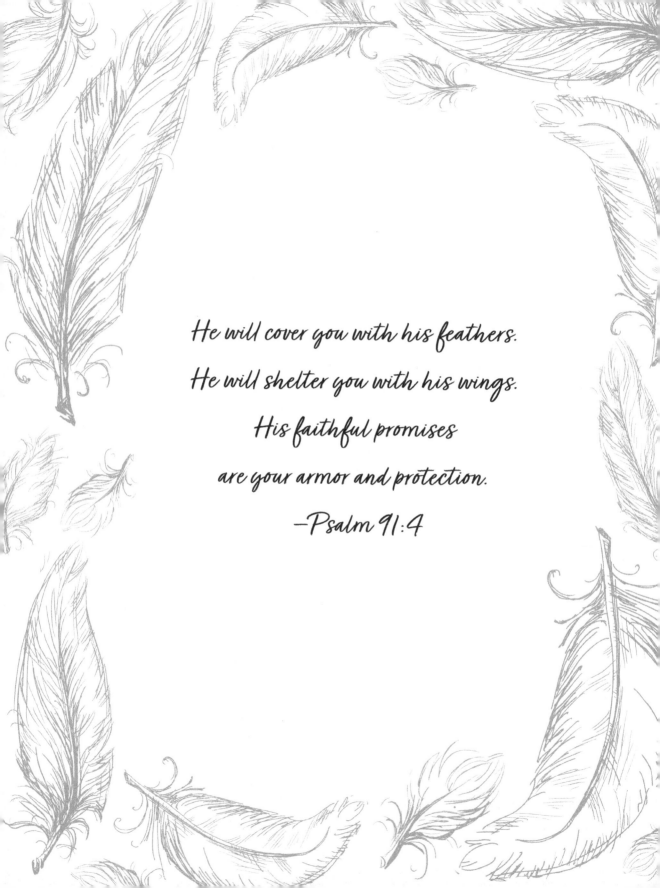

He will cover you with his feathers.

He will shelter you with his wings.

His faithful promises

are your armor and protection.

—Psalm 91:4

Introduction

He will cover you with his feathers. He will shelter you with his wings.
His faithful promises are your armor and protection. —Psalm 91:4

· · · · · · · · · · · · · · · ·

How is life going inside that head of yours? Are you quiet and peaceful, everything in harmony with contentment prevailing? Or are you a bit of a mess? Do you hear whispers that remind you of failure and shame? Do you feel paralyzed at times, unable to figure out what on earth you're supposed to do and why you're even here? Do you feel like you're flying against the wind, beaten back no matter how hard you flap your wings?

Regardless of your current situation, I have a big dream and prayer for you: that God will meet you in the pages of Scripture in a supernatural way, calling you to rest and peace, equipping you to fly and even to soar above the storm clouds, fulfilling the destiny He has for you.

That's not too much to ask, right? After all, He made you. He made you well. And He most definitely has good plans for you, whether you believe this or not. I'm inviting you on a journey to experience the sweet way God invades and changes our thoughts and our problems and our joys when we begin our day giving Him time and listening to Him.

I love the picture created in my mind by our theme verse: "He will cover you with his feathers. He will shelter you with his wings. His faithful promises are your armor and protection" (Psalm 91:4). When I read this, all of a sudden in my imagination (which is very active by the way), I'm a tiny bird, too small to fly. Yet I'm safe as can be because my Father has covered me with His strong and protective feathers. His wings protect me like armor, and I nestle down in peace.

The goal of this devotional book is based on that analogy—nestling in with your Heavenly Father, growing in your knowledge of Him, the real and living God who speaks to us through the Bible. You'll begin with a guided study and end feeling able and equipped to open the wonderful Word of God all on your own—hearing Him and learning from Him as you read. That's a big goal. It's a goal that will bless you and help sustain you all the days of your life. I'm thrilled to share this with you. *Oh, Lord, give us wings to fly and soar!*

This book is divided into three sections. We start out in the Nest. My hope is that as you go through the daily devotionals found there, you'll begin to feel the true safety and peace that comes from belonging to the God who loves you. Each lesson lays a foundation of trust that will ready you and steady you to try your wings.

The next section is called Flight. We'll transition from lessons on our safety and comfort as a child of God to a stretching of wings. We'll learn to "fly" as we practice a simple method of Bible study promoted by Sweet Selah Ministries. Each day will be a new adventure as we unpack a passage of Scripture, utilizing a profoundly effective system of devotional study. It's a flight tool that God has used to keep me soaring above many a storm cloud over the years, and I'm eager to share it with you. Honestly, once I learned this method, I was amazed at how rich and personal the reading of God's Word could be.

Finally, in our last section of the book, you'll Soar. You'll reach the goal when a devotional book isn't even necessary. You'll be meeting with God, just the two of you, on your own, learning to still yourself and hear Him speak, finding direction and guidance for your day. And when storm clouds come (and they will), this steady study of His Word will enable you to find joy even in trials as you meet with the God who still speaks to us today.

Each section will guide you a little further into a life journey that can be filled with both peace and adventure. Oh, you have an amazing future when you choose to put yourself under His wings! In the psalm below check out what God has to say about you . . . yes, specifically . . . you. But, before you do, here's what I recommend.

If you aren't sitting down, nice and comfortable, do that. Find a chair or bed or couch or patch of grass and sit your weary body down. Do you like tea? Coffee? Ice water? Grab a cup of whatever makes you smile. And then read this beautiful psalm out loud. Just read it. Imagine yourself as a little chick under the glorious and mighty wings of a good and competent God. Thank Him.

Those who live in the shelter of the Most High
will find rest in the shadow of the Almighty.
This I declare about the Lord:
He alone is my refuge, my place of safety;
he is my God, and I trust him.
For he will rescue you from every trap
and protect you from deadly disease.
He will cover you with his feathers.
He will shelter you with his wings.
His faithful promises are your armor and protection.

Do not be afraid of the terrors of the night,
nor the arrow that flies in the day.
Do not dread the disease that stalks in darkness,
nor the disaster that strikes at midday.
Though a thousand fall at your side,
though ten thousand are dying around you,
these evils will not touch you.
Just open your eyes,
and see how the wicked are punished.

If you make the LORD your refuge,
if you make the Most High your shelter,
no evil will conquer you;
no plague will come near your home.
For he will order his angels
to protect you wherever you go.
They will hold you up with their hands
so you won't even hurt your foot on a stone.
You will trample upon lions and cobras;
you will crush fierce lions and serpents under your feet!

The LORD says, "I will rescue those who love me.
I will protect those who trust in my name.
When they call on me, I will answer;
I will be with them in trouble.
I will rescue and honor them.
I will reward them with a long life
and give them my salvation."

—Psalm 91

Note from the author: Because this book is written with the purpose of helping women see that the Bible can be read by a complete novice with very little understanding of theology, I use the New Living Translation (NLT), a dynamic equivalence translation of the Bible, instead of a word-for-word translation for quoting most verses. The NLT is a reputable translation that is designed to be very readable and understandable. For more in-depth study of the Bible as you grow in your knowledge, I recommend you read other translations as well, such as the English Standard Version (ESV) or New American Standard (NASB) versions.

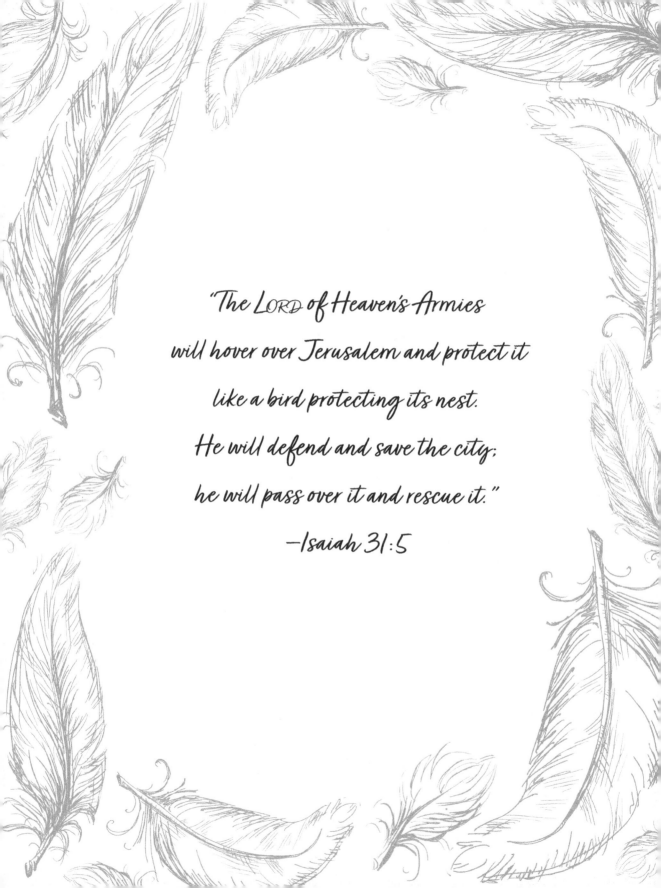

"The LORD of Heaven's Armies
will hover over Jerusalem and protect it
like a bird protecting its nest.
He will defend and save the city;
he will pass over it and rescue it."

—Isaiah 31:5

Nest

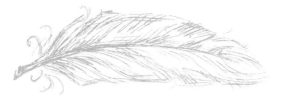

Nest Lessons Introduction

"The LORD of Heaven's Armies will hover over Jerusalem and protect it like a bird protecting its nest. He will defend and save the city; he will pass over it and rescue it." —Isaiah 31:5

. . . .

Once when I was a little girl, I got lost on a beach. It was a warm day and the crowds were large. We were in England visiting my grandparents at the time. My mother and grandparents had set up a place for us with chairs for the grownups and blankets for the children. We had a picnic lunch together, and all was jolly and good.

But then came the fog. I had run down to the water's edge, not far at all from the safety of our specially marked-out spot, feeling happy and joyful as I kicked at the water with my five-year-old feet. I must have wandered a bit because when I next looked up, a swirling fog was descending on the beach—nothing and no one looked at all familiar. I can still recall the stark panic of that moment. There I was in an unfamiliar spot on an unfamiliar beach in an unfamiliar country. Talk about panic!

I can't remember how long I wandered, looking vainly for the right blanket and chairs that held my own dear family, but it felt like forever. Finally, in the midst of my frantic searching and peering through the fog, I heard my mother's voice loud and high calling me home to "our" little nest in the sand. She held me closely as I trembled, and after that I stayed very close to that spot where I felt safe with the adults in my life who cared for me.

A nest is built for little ones, especially for birds and their eggs and babies. When I was a little one, that blanket haven on the beach looked like a safe little nest to me. When a baby bird first cracks through its shell all damp with feathers flat against its body, it needs a cupped and hidden home in which to grow. It can't fly. It can't even move much at first. Can't feed itself. Before long, though, it has learned to open that cute little beak wide and often, waiting for food to be dropped in by its parents. It gains strength day by day in its hidden place safe from predators. And if a predator does come, the parent will fight for its young with a puffed out chest and raucous cries. A nest represents a safe place with someone who will protect you.

For the next couple of weeks, you and I will spend a bit of Nest time together. We'll begin with some foundational lessons that will teach us—or remind us—who we are in

Christ and all the privileges we have of trusting and clinging and asking and relying on Him. As I've prayed about this book, I've asked God to show me what nourishment we most need. What lessons from God's Word will help us sprout and grow and stretch when our wings are weak? I'm eager for us to begin this journey, and I hope each "feeding" will give us a little less wobble in our step and a little more confidence as we prepare to fly.

I love the imagery in the verse we began with: "The Lord of Heaven's Armies will hover over Jerusalem and protect it like a bird protecting its nest. He will defend and save the city; he will pass over it and rescue it" (Isaiah 31:5). As we meet with God each day, we will be protected by His sure covering. If we've invited Him into our lives, He hovers over us with deep love and joy that we are His. Our God is so huge that He controls and commands the armies of Heaven. Imagine a host of angels all straight and tall and ready to do as He commands. This is the God who places His wings of protection around us as we seek Him! Pray with me for God's guidance as we prepare to jump into our very first devotional in the Nest.

Heavenly Father, please protect us as we start this journey of studying Your Word and seeking to know You better. Give us a strong sense of Your Presence as we nestle in for this time of learning and listening each day. Protect us from the enemy of our souls who will try to distract us and keep us from seeking You daily. Protect us from condemnation and feelings of inadequacy. Help us to rejoice that You love all Your little ones including the immature ones . . . the stumbling ones . . . the poor and the needy and the desperate. Hover over us in the nest, dear Lord, and help us learn to fly. In Jesus' Name, Amen.

Joining the Family of God

For those who aren't sure and want to know more . . .

For those Christians who love reading about joining God's family . . .

As we start this journey, I feel compelled to share with you how to become a member of God's family—just in case you don't feel you belong to Him. Oh, dear one. How He loves you and wants you to come to Him and be His child! Here's a simple explanation of what it means to become His.

1. Long ago the universe, including our planet Earth, animals, and humans, were all made by God. It didn't just happen by chance. The complexity and variety of the design and sheer wonder of creation points to a Someone who made it. God did.

2. God specifically made *you*. He chose the DNA that would become your wonderful self. He doesn't make duplicates. Every snowflake is unique and so is every human being.

The Bible says that He knit you together in your mother's womb (Psalm 139:13). He knew you before your first cry.

3. Every single one of us is born with what the Bible calls a "sin nature." The first humans, Adam and Eve, were created in perfection, but they chose disobedience to God and sin entered the world. This basically means that now even when we try to do what's good and want to do good, we're easily tempted and persuaded not to do good. We lie. We hurt feelings. We strike back in rage. We're jealous of others. We say hurtful things we wish we could take back. We are—every one of us—quite the mess. And this sin nature of ours often leads to feelings of depression and unworthiness and insignificance.

4. Sin separates us from God, and God, who knows all things, knew we would never be free from sin on our own. Yet His heart of love for His creation—for you and me—was to restore relationship. So, at a specific time in history, He entered it. God Himself, clothed in a human body, came and walked on earth. His human name as God the Son . . . is Jesus. By His life He revealed to us the very nature of God the Father. Jesus healed the sick, He raised the dead, and He taught us what love means by word and action. The Bible records His story, as do many other reliable historical sources from that period.

5. Why did He have to die? Even we humans have an innate sense in us that sin needs punishment. That's why we have jails for adults and time outs for children. In fact, when we do what's stupidly wrong, we grow so dismayed with ourselves that we often self punish by repeated angry, disgusted thoughts and guilty feelings. In His great love, Jesus was willing to pay the death penalty for our sins and take the punishment we deserved. As God in human form, He chose to suffer an agonizing and humiliating death on a Roman cross for you and me. And God accepted His sacrifice. When we ask God, He fully forgives all our sin. He no longer sees our sin, but sees it paid in full by His Son, Jesus.

6. Jesus did not stay dead! This is the astounding truth and good news of the Christian faith. Death could not hold Him, and He is alive today. After the crucifixion, over 500 people literally saw Jesus walking and talking, and many of them were willing to be killed rather than deny they had seen Him alive after His death. Many Jesus followers were ordered to turn from Christianity in those early days. They were fed to lions and lit like torches in Rome. And thousands of them chose painful deaths, because they knew they had seen God risen from the grave—and they knew that after death, they would live with Him.

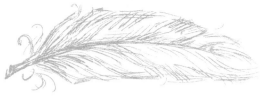

7. Yes, that is the incredibly Good News! Jesus died and rose again, taking our sin on Himself and conquering death for all time.

8. You are offered this gift of forgiveness, love, and relationship with God Himself along with everyone else on this planet. "For God so loved the world that He gave His only begotten Son, that whoever believes in Him should not perish but have everlasting life" (John 3:16 NKJV). You are one of the billions of "whoevers" to whom He whispers, "Believe in Me and what I did for you and live."

9. That's truly all you need to know to be free from sin, clean, forgiven, and ready to step into new life as God's legally adopted child. Our great God longs for you to turn to Him and trust that what Jesus did as a sacrifice for you was sufficient to bring you into His wonderful family. If you wish to respond to His call, pray the words printed below or create your own words. God promises that those who seek Him will find Him. Trust in that.

Sample Prayer

Dear God, I long to belong to You. I am thoroughly ashamed of my sins and all the times I've ignored You, the One who made me. Please forgive me and have mercy on me. I trust in Jesus and believe that His death and resurrection paved the way for me to have everlasting life. Please, God, take me as Your child as I receive You as my Savior and Lord. Enter into me and my life and dwell with me that I might know You better and love You more. Thank You for a love so big You would die for me. I choose You, and I want to be Your child. In Jesus' Name, Amen.

Dear new sister (or brother!) in Christ,

If you prayed that prayer with even the tiniest bit of faith, God heard. God answered. God welcomed you. May you come to know Him better and better day by day from now until you cross from death to life everlasting with Him. The Nest lessons that follow will help you begin to grow in your walk with Jesus. Find a good church home where the people who attend believe in Jesus and His saving death and resurrection.

And! Would you please write to me? I'd love to pray for you and help you find a church if you don't have one. Seriously. I have no greater joy on the planet than to know that you and others like you have found your home with the One who made you and loves you best of all. You can reach me at sharon@sweetselah.org.

Love and welcome to the family,

Sharon

In this is love,
not that we loved God
but that he loved us
and sent his Son to be
the atoning sacrifice
for our sins.
— 1 John 4:10

Rest in His Love

In this is love, not that we loved God but that he loved us and sent his
Son to be the atoning sacrifice for our sins. — 1 John 4:10 NRSV

• • • • • • • • • • • • • • • • • •

Aren't you grateful that God's love for you doesn't ebb and flow like your love for Him? I sure am. Some days I can't contain myself. I want to shout out my love for Him and belt out all my favorite praise songs. Sadly, some days I totally shut Him out, sitting in my own self-made funk of self-pity and blah. On those bad days, how I need verses like the one above from 1 John. God makes it very clear over and over in the Bible that He just plain loves us. He loves us whether we return His love or not. That is super comforting to grasp.

The problem is, we don't easily grasp it. We know ourselves. Not just the smiling, presentable self we show to people each day. We know the dark side that judges others, prefers her own comfort over service to others, who, quite frankly, at times wishes the world and everyone in it would just go away for a bit and let her do what she wants, thank you very much. Inherently, each of us is selfish to the core. Our own comfort, our own needs, our own hurts are magnified in our minds—and if we are not walking with God, that selfishness can eclipse everything else. We are not very nice to be around. [Deep. Sigh.]

And yet He loves us. He loves me. He loves you. He does. Today's Nest assignment is to begin—now—to believe this startling truth. You are not some exception to the rule. There are no exceptions. God . . . Loves . . . You. Deeply. Here are a few verses that give us insight into God's heart and all He has to say about His love for even His wayward ones.

. . . He [God] has sent me [Jesus] to bind up the brokenhearted, to proclaim liberty to the captives and the opening of the prison to those who are bound. —Isaiah 61:1b ESV

But when the kindness of God our Savior and His love for mankind appeared, He saved us, not on the basis of deeds which we have done in righteousness, but according to His mercy . . . —Titus 3:4-5a NASB

For I am persuaded that neither death nor life, nor angels nor principalities nor powers, nor things present nor things to come, nor height nor depth, nor any other created thing, shall be able to separate us from the love of God which is in Christ Jesus our Lord. —Romans 8:38-39 NKJV

The steadfast love of the LORD never ceases, his mercies never come to an end; they are new every morning; great is your faithfulness. —Lamentations 3:22-23 NRSV

My Reflections

Is it hard for you to believe that you are loved? Write a short letter to God telling Him why. Or if you know right down to your pinky toe that you are dearly loved by Him, write Him a letter about that "knowing" and how grateful you are.

Reread the four verses that speak of His love. Pick your favorite and write it out here, thinking about each precious word as you write.

Write out a prayer, your response to God from that beautiful verse. Don't worry about how it sounds. Keep it as simple as you like. Even a short little "thank You for Your love" would be enough. Just let Him know that you appreciate His love—the love of the One who made you and who gave His life for you. Yes, He cares for you that much!

You, dear one, are deeply, fully loved.

"Don't be afraid of those who want to kill your body; they cannot touch your soul. . . . What is the price of two sparrows—one copper coin? But not a single sparrow can fall to the ground without your Father knowing it. And the very hairs on your head are all numbered. So don't be afraid; you are more valuable to God than a whole flock of sparrows."

—Matthew 10:28a, 29-31

Trust in His Care

"Don't be afraid of those who want to kill your body; they cannot touch your soul. . . . What is the price of two sparrows—one copper coin? But not a single sparrow can fall to the ground without your Father knowing it. And the very hairs on your head are all numbered. So don't be afraid; you are more valuable to God than a whole flock of sparrows." —Matthew 10:28a, 29-31

• • • • • • • • • • • • • • • • • •

Have you ever asked God . . . actually begged God . . . for a heart's desire and yet *not* received what you felt you so desperately needed? I have. It hurts when you run to God in despair, asking Him to help, knowing He is perfectly able to help, and then seeing the very thing you feared most come to be. I've prayed for people to live and instead they have died. I've prayed for marriages to be saved and they ended in divorce. I've prayed for a loved one to find Christ and watched him walk farther and farther away. I bet you have too.

And yet here I am telling you with confidence that if you belong to God, you can trust in His care. Yes, you can. Read the first line of our verse again and linger on His solid promise. No matter what happens to your body or to the body of someone you love, God's got your soul. Permanently. Irrevocably. Foreverly. I know that's not a word, but I want to use it anyway. Because that's the kind of love God has for you. A forever love. Rock solid. Even in pain He has a purpose that He is working for your good, not your harm.

Do you know how many sparrows exist in this world? The most common of all the birds, they can be found on every continent except Antarctica. The conservation group, Partners in Flight, estimates there are over 540 million of them. Five hundred forty million! So basically, they're pretty common and run of the mill. Yet God knows every one. He sees when one little bird falls to the ground. He cares. He notices. You might feel like an insignificant run-of-the-mill sparrow-type yourself. Guess what? God loves run-of-the-mill sparrow-types. In fact, He thinks each one of us is so special and unique that He has even bothered to count the number of hairs on our heads . . . each one of us, personally.

You can trust God. You can trust Him when things go your way and every prayer you pray is answered with a resounding, "Yes!" You can trust His "No, dear one," as well.

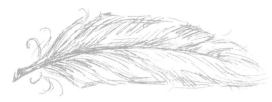

He has your soul. He has the very heart of you, and He will never, ever let you go. When the tough times come, He doesn't leave you. He's right there in the midst, aching with you, but also knowing that this hard thing is being woven together for good into the beautiful tapestry He is making of your life.

The amazing story of Joseph in the Bible is a perfect one for teaching us this truth that God works for good in even the worst of situations. Joseph's brothers plotted to kill him—how's that for family love? Instead, they sold him as a slave to a country far away from home with no prospect of ever seeing his father again. Overcoming incredible obstacles, he became the competent manager of a rich man's estate, but then due to a slanderous lie, he was tossed into prison. Again, he worked his way up to a position of trust even in prison and had the opportunity to ask another prisoner to say a good word for him. Once again, hope was dashed when that prisoner, upon his release, promptly forgot all about Joseph, who lingered in prison another two years. One heart-breaking incident after another for a Very Long Time. Yet in every situation, Joseph leaned on God, and God had his soul. Through the hardest of times regardless of the circumstances, Joseph continued to trust God. In the end, his life took a dramatic turn when he became second in command in all of Egypt, as well as a husband and a father. Oh, and he also saved the world from starvation and ended up reconciling with his own family in the process. It's one great story of triumph despite suffering.

In all the hard times I've faced, I've been able to see—later on down the road—how God has used each one for a good purpose. I've been able to comfort others with understanding because I've hurt too. I've seen a strengthening of character and purpose in many who have been knocked down but who have still trusted God. I've experienced His Presence in the midst of suffering in ways I know I would never have if times had always been good. Trust in His care for you. He will be with you in every trial. Lean on Him.

My Reflections

Read Genesis 45. It's the happy ending part of Joseph's story. Write down what you see in Joseph's words that reveal his abiding trust in God.

Pick a favorite verse from this chapter and write it out so you can see it and examine it. What makes that verse special to you? If you like to doodle, make the verse all fancy. If not . . . just write it. Either way, writing will help you remember it.

Pray. Join me in this prayer or pray your own words.

Dear God, help me to comprehend Your words of assurance to me. You notice even little sparrows, and I am much more valuable to You than they. You count every hair on my head, Lord. You know me. And You hold my soul. No one can touch it. Help me to trust that Your plans for me are good. Help me to look for You and what You are doing even in the hardest of times. Thank You that You never leave me. I love that I am Yours forever. In Jesus' Name, Amen.

Rest in this. You are of great value to the King of kings.

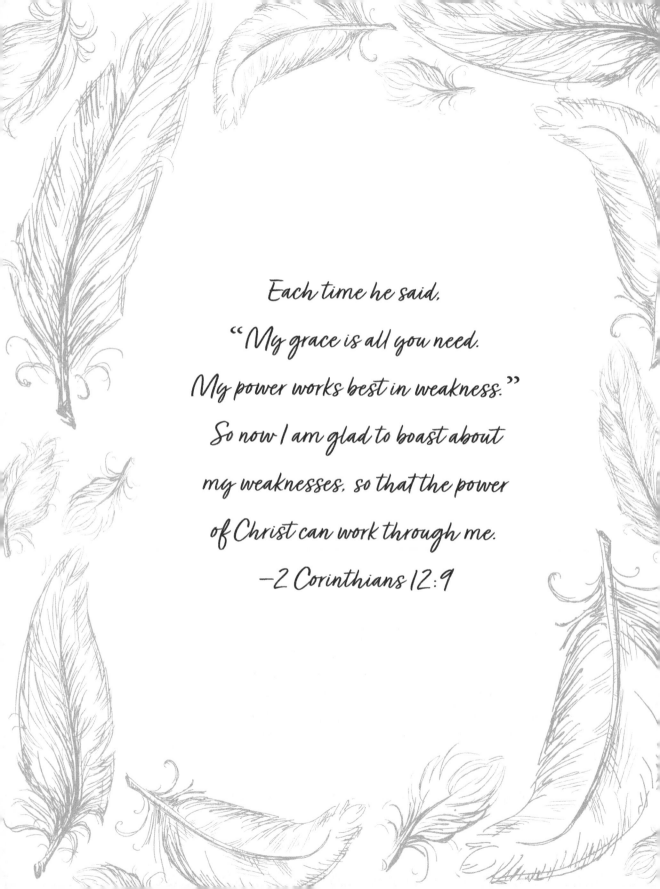

Each time he said,
"My grace is all you need.
My power works best in weakness."
So now I am glad to boast about
my weaknesses, so that the power
of Christ can work through me.

—2 Corinthians 12:9

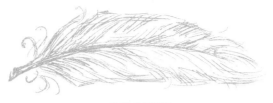

Rely on His Strength

Each time he said, "My grace is all you need. My power works best in weakness." So now I am glad to boast about my weaknesses, so that the power of Christ can work through me. —2 Corinthians 12:9

. . . .

"I can't do it anymore," I whispered in the dark. I was staying at my father-in-law's and caregiving, caregiving, caregiving. After a leg amputation, he could not walk or even stand, and I was the one responsible for him. Running his household, attempting to run my own from a distance, trying to learn a Hoyer lift, I felt drained, heavy, and so, so weak. It was a struggle to even pray. But there I was, lying on a makeshift bed, hoping to sleep because the alarm would wake me in three hours to shift his position to prevent bedsores. It all seemed completely impossible.

I prayed pitiful little prayers that night while my heart raced and my mind whirred. Simple prayers like, "help me" and "I feel lost, Lord" and "I can't do this anymore." I cried, tears leaking from my eyes. I didn't even have the energy to sob, so the tears just dribbled. After a while, I drifted off to sleep.

When the alarm went off, I turned my father-in-law and slept again another three hours. When I finally got up, made my tea, sat with my Bible, and prayed for strength for the day . . . I was astounded to realize . . . I actually had strength. It was kind of miraculous. I was able to love my father-in-law and deal with the nurses and aides with a measure of joy I had been sorely lacking (extra-miraculous). God in His grace had answered my pitiful, mewling cries for help with a strength that was clearly from Him. It was a glorious day.

No one wants to go through a time of extreme weakness. I surely didn't. But I can testify to you, dear reader, that when you are at the very, very end of your own strength the reality of God's strength will manifest itself in a mighty way. The power and joy I had that day came from God. Not me. And like Paul, I'm glad I was weak, because it allowed me to see how strong He is!

Oftentimes since, I have jokingly reminded God of 2 Corinthians 12:9. "Lord, I'm weak again. So . . . yay! It's time for You to show Your power and help me go forth in Your strength."

It makes me smile to think about it. Yes! At my very weakest, I'm not yet undone. For it's just at that breaking point when God's glory shines through in a breathtaking way! In an earlier section of his letter to the Corinthians, Paul had shared with wonder how God was there for him and those with him during crazy trials:

> For God, who said, "Let there be light in the darkness," has made this light shine in our hearts so we could know the glory of God that is seen in the face of Jesus Christ. We now have this light shining in our hearts, but we ourselves are like fragile clay jars containing this great treasure. This makes it clear that our great power is from God, not from ourselves. We are pressed on every side by troubles, but we are not crushed. We are perplexed, but not driven to despair. We are hunted down, but never abandoned by God. We get knocked down, but we are not destroyed.
> —2 Corinthians 4:6-9

It's incredibly true. Even at our weakest, God is there with new strength. We don't have to be the strong ones. We simply have to confess our need to Him in simple, desperate prayers. And then watch how He gives us supernatural ability to cope.

My favorite part of the passage above? "We are never abandoned by God." May His strength show forth in you on the days you are weakest. And remember too that He supplies all our needs for each day. We are wise to rely on His strength, not our own, even on those days when we feel we have it all together. Let's celebrate that we have the Holy Spirit within us to help us in the toughest times—and all the time! We are blessed.

My Reflections

Read Isaiah 40:25-31. These seven little verses are packed with wonder and truth. Consider reading them out loud so that you catch every meaningful word. Write out your favorite verse from this passage.

Write a prayer and share with God why you love this verse.

If you are in a situation that has you feeling weak, pray right now and ask God to give you His strength to replace your weakness. And then rest in Him and wait. You will see His good hand at work in your life.

Rejoice in knowing that He will pour His strength into you today.

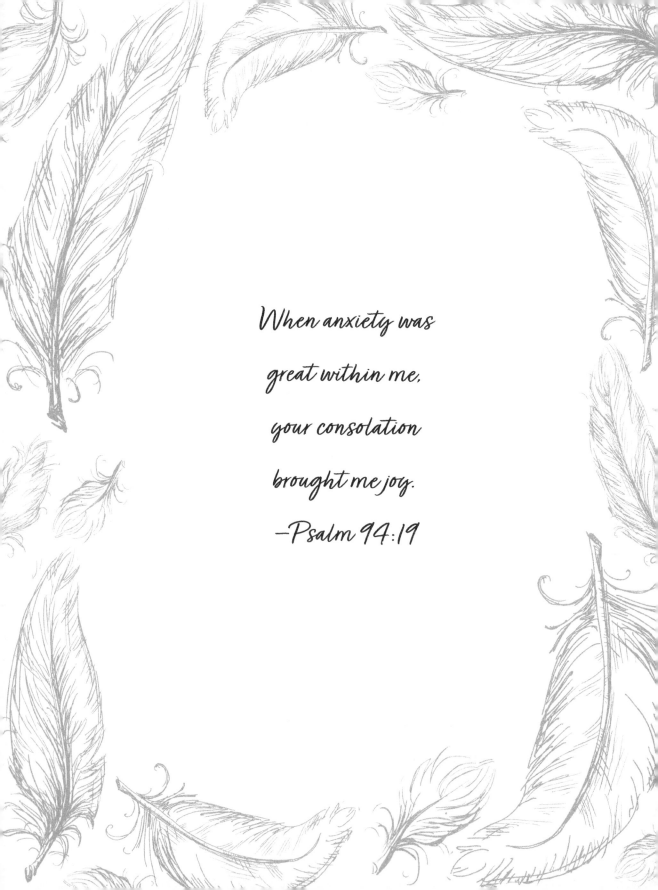

When anxiety was
great within me,
your consolation
brought me joy.
—Psalm 94:19

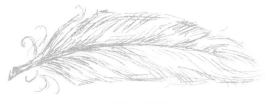

Bring Him Your Anxiety

When anxiety was great within me, your consolation
brought me joy. —Psalm 94:19 NIV

• • • • • • • • • • • • • • • • • • • •

Anxiety can strike at the most bizarre moments. My father and I were in the rather sleepy downtown area of my city, Dover, New Hampshire, where I was helping him buy a new telescope. We managed to settle it safely in the back of his station wagon, and Dad began backing the car out of the area behind the shop. He was going probably two miles an hour. No other cars or people were obstructing the way. Yet when he started to back up, I absolutely panicked. My heart raced. My breathing was shallow as my throat constricted. My eyes flared in terror. Wait. What?! I was in a state of all-out panic because my father was slowly backing up a car? What was wrong with me? Even I could in no way justify the level of terror brought on by such a simple, everyday activity—and this was just one in a series of similar events that finally led me to admit I had a problem and needed help.

I wish I had read this verse back then. Because, you see, when you're a Christian and have the Holy Spirit literally living within you and guiding you, you feel mighty ashamed that you can't be calm and peaceful all the time. Satan loves to attack the weak and vulnerable. One of his biggest lies is that God's response to people who are anxious and nervous is disgust or disdain or even anger. That, my friend, is a lie. Read this beautiful verse and rest in it. *When anxiety is great within you . . . God consoles.* And His consolation brings—not condemnation—but *joy*. God doesn't want you . . . or me . . . trapped in an anxious cycle of terror and fear—and He will not add to our anguish when we suffer. His perfect love casts out fear. He brings no torment. He brings consolation. Wow. How blessed we are to be His!

That little incident in the car was the beginning of a journey for me, a journey of seeking to be a calmer and less frazzled human being. Many component parts led to my particular healing journey, and if you suffer from anxiety attacks, your journey will likely be very different from mine. So with compassion I share what I have learned and hope it will be helpful. At the same time, I know you are uniquely wired and might need

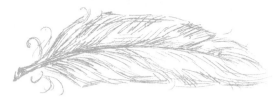

different strategies. In any case, as you seek healing, do remember that your God consoles and holds you. You can run to Him when you're anxious, knowing His response will always be kind and loving and gentle.

Here are some of the ways God helped me cope with anxiety, which I'm grateful to say is . . . gone. Totally gone. No more anxiety attacks!

- ❧ He called me to more rest and less striving.
- ❧ He taught me to pray through the anxiety.
- ❧ He gave me scriptures to battle the enemy who wanted to keep me bound.
- ❧ He reminded me that His love for me does not depend on my emotions. His love for me is always, always surrounding me.

If you do not suffer from anxiety, pray for those who do and be tender with them. If you do suffer from anxiety, don't hesitate to seek out the advice of your doctor. And do seek God's help and His consolation in the midst of it. Bring your anxiety to Him. Don't let lies keep you far from Him at the time you need Him most desperately.

My Reflections

Read these verses and write down at least one practical way to rest more and strive less.

This is what the Sovereign LORD, the Holy One of Israel, says: "In repentance and rest is your salvation, in quietness and trust is your strength, but you would have none of it. You said, 'No, we will flee on horses.' Therefore you will flee! You said, 'We will ride off on swift horses.' Therefore your pursuers will be swift! A thousand will flee at the threat of one; at the threat of five you will all flee away, till you are left like a flagstaff on a mountaintop, like a banner on a hill." —Isaiah 30:15-17 NIV

Read these verses and write down what God promises if we pray through the anxiety.

Do not be anxious about anything, but in every situation, by prayer and petition, with thanksgiving, present your requests to God. And the peace of God, which transcends all understanding, will guard your hearts and your minds in Christ Jesus. —Philippians 4:6-7 NIV

Choose one of these verses and memorize it. Use your verse as a weapon to battle the enemy with God's Word when he attacks.

There is no fear in love. But perfect love drives out fear because fear has to do with punishment. The one who fears is not made perfect in love. —1 John 4:18 NIV

For the Spirit God gave us does not make us timid, but gives us power, love and self-discipline. —2 Timothy 1:7 NIV

Cast all your anxiety on him because he cares for you. —1 Peter 5:7 NIV

Before you go to bed tonight, I suggest you read this wonderful passage of Scripture out loud again. In fact, maybe write it out on a note card or on your phone and read it often throughout the day. Soak in it until it becomes dearly familiar.

For I am convinced that neither death nor life, neither angels nor demons, neither the present nor the future, nor any powers, neither height nor depth, nor anything else in all creation, will be able to separate us from the love of God that is in Christ Jesus our Lord. —Romans 8:38-39 NIV

His love for you always, always surrounds you.

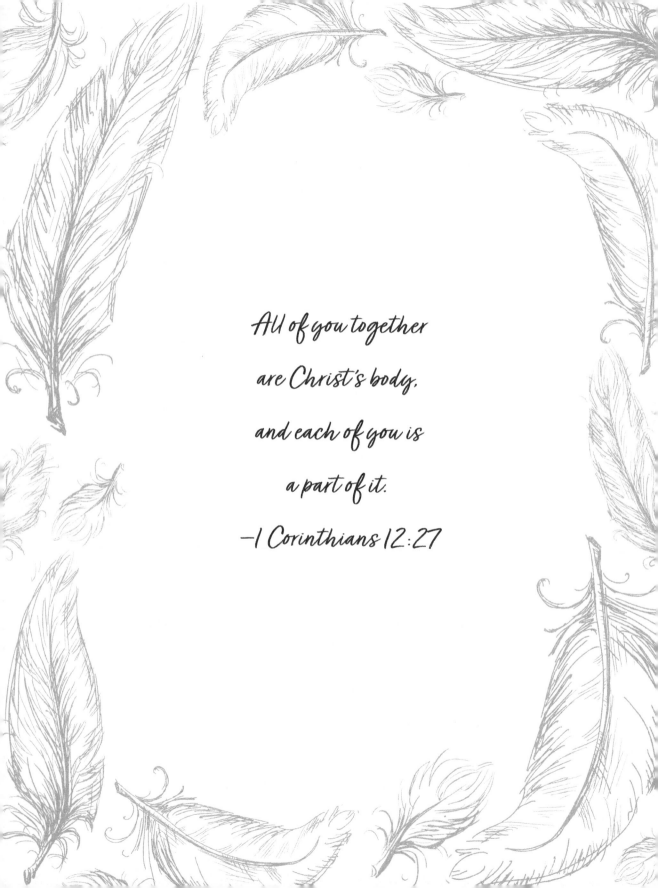

All of you together
are Christ's body,
and each of you is
a part of it.

—1 Corinthians 12:27

Reject Comparison

All of you together are Christ's body, and each of you
is a part of it. —1 Corinthians 12:27

• • • • • • • • • • • • • • • • • •

There was a time in my life when I longed to be someone else. I'll call her Ashley. She was beautiful and blonde with a petite and perfect nose. I was a gawky brunette with a (much) larger nose that made me self-conscious. Ashley was everything I was not. Quiet and self-controlled, she smiled warmly and invitingly. She listened more than she talked. She was calm. I was a storm. I had a hard time being quiet, talking more than I listened. I felt everything deeply and often reacted with more intensity than was comfortable for those around me. Ashley glided through life. I raced, bumping into things as I rounded corners way too fast.

I actually tried to be like Ashley. I'd practice her slow, gentle, gracious ways while holding my tongue between my teeth. To some degree, I did need to tone it down, but the bottom line is: God made me . . . me. He didn't want me to be Ashley. He made Ashley beautifully, but He also made me beautifully. He wired Ashley for quiet and comfort. He wired me for speaking out and encouraging. Both of us are needed.

How are you doing at liking you? Are you able to look at yourself and believe and trust that the temperament you have is a gift from a good God? Can you receive the body features He placed in you that are a bit more (or less) than you might wish? Oh, how it pleases God, the Creator, when we accept the way He has made us with a grateful heart. We are unique in this world and dearly loved by Him.

Making comparisons is a subtle rejection of what God has chosen for me. When I yearn to be like someone else or to have what someone else has, I turn my head away from the path God has laid out for me. God says quite clearly in Scripture that we are not to "covet." To covet means to yearn or crave for something you do not have that often belongs to someone else (a Sharon definition). Do you know what happens when we are caught comparing ourselves with others?

❧ We start disliking those "others," instead of loving them and being there for them.
❧ We neglect gratitude. We stop noticing all the good gifts God has given us.

- We elevate lesser things, like a smaller nose or a bigger house, over things that matter, like sharing Jesus with a lost and dying world.
- We become depressed and dissatisfied, instead of happy and eager to serve.
- We are distracted from the mission God has for us.

The consequences of comparison are pretty much horrid, aren't they? So. Don't do it. Don't go there. And when you do? Just as soon as you recognize what's happening, walk away. A great antidote for comparison is gratitude. Do you wish you had a body like someone else's? Start thanking God for how He made that someone else, asking Him to bless her and use her for His glory. Then thank God for what He has given you: lungs that work, legs that move, eyes that see. Do you wish you had talents like someone else? Turn to prayer and thank God for her and ask God to use her. Humbly ask God to show you ways He can use you and thank Him for making you just as He did. As 1 Corinthians 12:27 says, each of you is a part of Christ's body. You, dear one, are needed and necessary just the way God made you. He fashioned you with love and great purpose. Rest in that.

My Reflections

Read 1 Corinthians 12:12-27 and summarize it here. What do you learn about yourself from this passage?

Pick a favorite verse and write it out. Then write the reasons it was your choice.

Pray with me, and then continue in your own words.

Dear Father God, forgive me when I yearn for other things instead of noticing what I do have. Turn my heart away from comparison. Help me "see" why You have made me just as I am. Help me turn comparison thoughts into prayers that reflect a grateful heart instead of a coveting heart. Oh, Lord God! You do all things well. Thank You for making me as You have. Please fulfill Your purposes for my life in and through me. [Continue talking to God in your own words.]

You are a precious treasure fashioned with care by the one true God.

For since our friendship
with God was restored by
the death of his Son while we
were still his enemies, we will
certainly be saved through the life
of his Son. So now we can rejoice
in our wonderful new relationship
with God because our Lord
Jesus Christ has made us
friends of God.
–Romans 5:10-11

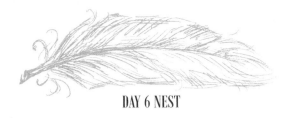

Be Amazed at His Friendship

For since our friendship with God was restored by the death of his Son while
we were still his enemies, we will certainly be saved through the life of his Son.
So now we can rejoice in our wonderful new relationship with God because
our Lord Jesus Christ has made us friends of God. —Romans 5:10-11

• • • • • • • • • • • • • • • • • •

I am humbled and awed by these verses. How can it be that God considers me a
friend? According to Google Dictionary, a friend is "a person whom one knows and with
whom one has a bond of mutual affection." Friends are those who like you and want to
spend time with you. The ones who listen to your woes and cheer your victories. Friends
are loyal. They defend you. They tell you their secrets. Friends are a treasure and good
friends that "stick" are hard to find. And yet in these verses we discover that through
Christ's work on the cross, we have the grand privilege of being God's *friends*.

What worth He gives you if you belong to Him! It's stunning really. We celebrate
that today as we look at God's words line by line and marvel.

For since our friendship with God was restored. This joyous friendship is actually
what God planned from the beginning when He created human beings. He spent
time with Adam and Eve. They walked together in the Garden of Eden at the end
of each day, sharing thoughts and news. God always intended for us to be His companions. His friends.

By the death of his Son while we were still his enemies. The stunning fact is . . . He
loved you so deeply even while you were His enemy—not caring about Him at all
and actively living a life contrary to His wishes—He died for you. He died for me.
He chose to take all our sin on Himself and take the punishment we deserve in our
place. Oh, how He loves us, and His love for us gives us infinite worth and value!

We will certainly be saved through the life of his Son. He saved us. Pure and simple.
Please recognize God's amazing love for you. He sent Jesus to earth to rescue you.
Yes, you. You are not an exception. John 3:16 tells us God so loved the world . . .
and you are certainly in this world so . . . He. Loves. You. And He came to save you.
What love! What grace!*

* If you have not yet received this saving love, or if you have doubts about it, turn to page 15 in this book and learn how
you can become His child and a true "friend of God."

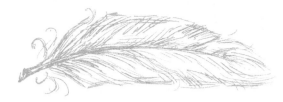

So now we can rejoice in our wonderful new relationship with God because our Lord Jesus Christ has made us friends of God. This is, indeed, worthy of rejoicing! Oh, be happy that you have a forever friend in Christ. This new relationship that is ours when we turn to Him and accept His great gift of salvation is a forever relationship. He will always love you. He will always want your companionship. He will. And someday you and I will have the joy of seeing Him face to face. He is so big and so awesome, and He is able to love each one of us uniquely and dearly throughout eternity. God. Our friend. Wow.

My Reflections

Read the passage below, Romans 5:1-12, and underline or circle each phrase that demonstrates God's great love for you.

Therefore, since we have been made right in God's sight by faith, we have peace with God because of what Jesus Christ our Lord has done for us. Because of our faith, Christ has brought us into this place of undeserved privilege where we now stand, and we confidently and joyfully look forward to sharing God's glory.

We can rejoice, too, when we run into problems and trials, for we know that they help us develop endurance. And endurance develops strength of character, and character strengthens our confident hope of salvation. And this hope will not lead to disappointment. For we know how dearly God loves us, because he has given us the Holy Spirit to fill our hearts with his love.

When we were utterly helpless, Christ came at just the right time and died for us sinners. Now, most people would not be willing to die for an upright person, though someone might perhaps be willing to die for a person who is especially good. But God showed his great love for us by sending Christ to die for us while we were still sinners. And since we have been made right in God's sight by the blood of Christ, he will certainly save us from God's condemnation. For since our friendship with God was restored by the death of his Son while we were still his enemies, we will certainly be saved through the life of his Son. So now we can rejoice in our wonderful new relationship with God because our Lord Jesus Christ has made us friends of God.

Write a prayer thanking God for loving you that much.

God wants to be your friend. Rejoice in that wonderful thought!

In his grace, God has given us

different gifts for doing certain things well.

So if God has given you the ability to prophesy,

speak out with as much faith as God has given you. If your

gift is serving others, serve them well. If you are a teacher,

teach well. If your gift is to encourage others, be encouraging.

If it is giving, give generously. If God has given you

leadership ability, take the responsibility seriously.

And if you have a gift for showing

kindness to others, do it gladly.

—Romans 12:6-8

Embrace Your Gifts

In his grace, God has given us different gifts for doing certain things well. So if God has given you the ability to prophesy, speak out with as much faith as God has given you. If your gift is serving others, serve them well. If you are a teacher, teach well. If your gift is to encourage others, be encouraging. If it is giving, give generously. If God has given you leadership ability, take the responsibility seriously. And if you have a gift for showing kindness to others, do it gladly. —Romans 12:6-8

• • • • • • • • • • • • • • • • • •

I wasn't actually even thinking about spiritual gifts that day as I walked with my friend. She and I met daily, Monday through Friday, to walk and talk in the early hours before work. On that particular day, she had spiritual gifts on her mind. "Sharon, as I have been studying gifts, I think I know what yours are—teaching and evangelism." Oh? Well then. Perhaps they are! I filed this away and pretty much ignored what she had said. God had to speak yet again to get my attention.

A few days later a letter arrived from a dear friend in Massachusetts. Out of the blue. I mean, I hadn't heard from her in a couple of months. She had just attended a weekend conference on spiritual gifts and loved her time there. She wrote about all she had learned and was most eager to share with me her conviction that my spiritual gifts were teaching and evangelism. What?! Twice in one week, two close friends with no prompting at all from me? This time, I woke up and paid attention.

In thinking about this, it seemed to me that God had used this unique fashion of communication, because these are "in front of people" gifts. He wanted to make very sure I knew that they were . . . gifts.

The Google Dictionary defines "gift" this way, "A thing given willingly to someone without payment; a present."

Do I have anything at all to do with a gift? Did I make it, wrap it, design it, or deliver it? Nope. I just received it. So . . . may I boast about a gift/present created for me and given to me by the Creator? Nope. It's a sweet, unearned, happy "thing given willingly to someone without payment."

I love teaching! I love evangelism! I want to use them for my King. And when

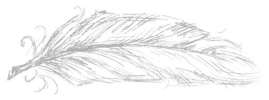

I bow my head and ask Him to work through me in these areas . . . He does. For His glory and for the furthering of His Kingdom. What an honor to work for the King of kings!

Here's the thing about spiritual gifts. As children of God, every single one of us has at least one. What about you? How are you wired? Both Romans 12 and 1 Corinthians 12 list a ton of various gifts. Did you notice that among those listed in Romans 12 above are the gifts of "encouragement" and "showing kindness?" Yup. These are gifts from God. Not everyone knows how to intuitively encourage another. Not everyone has a heart that melts when someone is hurting. But . . . maybe that's you. Or are you the organizing type? Are you great at keeping things tidy and in order? I suspect your church could use your help in some way.

Oh, friend, working in the area of your gifting is *joy*. "The place God calls you to," writes Frederick Buechner, "is the place where your deep gladness and the world's deep hunger meet."

Embrace your gifts. And then, head bowed, ask God to use them for His glory. You will find a "deep gladness" when you do.

My Reflections

Read Romans 12:4-13 and 1 Corinthians 12:4-31. Write out every gift mentioned. Then go back and circle the ones you believe God has given you.

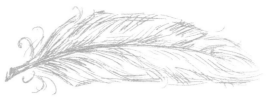

Ask God to reveal your gifts to you. Ask a trusted Christian friend or mentor what they believe your gifts are.

Let's pray.

Dear Father, thank You for giving us work to do that is meaningful and rich. Help me to hear You, Lord, in this area of spiritual gifting. Please show me my gifts so that I can use them for Your glory and Your Kingdom work. Please lead, guide, and direct me in this. Thank You for all You give! In Jesus' Name, Amen.

You have at least one amazing gift from God.
And you are a gift to those He's called you to love and serve.

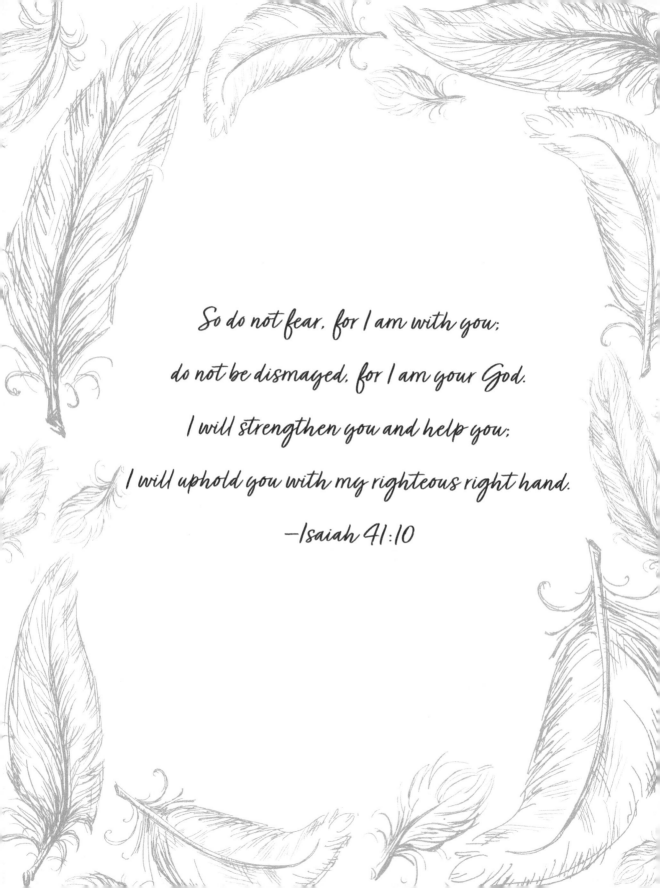

So do not fear, for I am with you;

do not be dismayed, for I am your God.

I will strengthen you and help you;

I will uphold you with my righteous right hand.

—Isaiah 41:10

Cling to His Hand

So do not fear, for I am with you; do not be dismayed, for I am
your God. I will strengthen you and help you; I will uphold you
with my righteous right hand. —Isaiah 41:10 NIV

• • • • • • • • • • • • • • • • • • • •

When I was a little girl, our family traveled to Great Britain every few years. That's because my mother is from England, and we had many lovely relatives to visit in that wonderful country. We usually flew into London's Heathrow Airport, which was huge even then. Upon arrival, we'd totter out of the plane worn and tired and half asleep and go collect our luggage. I remember feeling overwhelmed with the strangeness of it all. People talked with funny accents. And hundreds of them were moving about hauling their own belongings and bumping into little me. I knew instinctively that if I were to be separated from my family, I would be lost. Hopelessly, terribly, irrevocably lost.

So I clung to my mum or dad's hand. Tightly. Based on their firm grip, they obviously felt the same way. As we rushed through the airport, new sights and sounds assaulting my tired little mind, I remember feeling secure as long as my hand was safely encased by a parent's hand. It didn't matter where we were going or what strangeness awaited us. My parent was right there. I could feel and touch that hand. I would be okay.

Since then, I've experienced difficult times in life when I needed to be reminded that God's righteous right hand upholds me. There is no place on the planet I can go that He is not with me, right there, ready to strengthen me and help me. I can remember one particularly hard season when I stumbled upon the verse above—and I did cling to it just like I would to a physical hand. In fact, I imagined my little hand in His big and competent one. And I cried out, "Please don't let go. I'm lost and I'm bewildered and I don't know which way to go. But if You will hold my hand, I'll be okay."

What about you? When you're struggling with one issue or another—and struggle is actually pretty normal—do you reach for His hand? Try it. Take out that rusty imagination of yours and "see" God's good hand upholding you—because that is the absolute truth. He does that for you! He understands fear and promises, "I am with you." He gets it. At times you will be dismayed, so He assures you, "I am your God." What a good, good

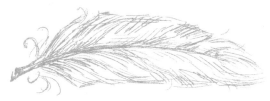

Father He is! He knows we will go through scary times, so in His Word He speaks reassurance to His kids. Believe what He says. Hold on tightly to the One who will never let you go!

My Reflections

Can you remember a "hand-holding" time from your childhood? Who was a trustworthy adult in your little life? (If you had no one . . . oh, I just want to hug you.) I hope at least one person in your life reached out a hand you trusted. Write their name down here and thank God for them.

Read Isaiah 41:13-20. What verse stirs your heart? Write it out here.

Time to pray. I invite you to write a short thank you to the One who holds your hand. If you find yourself in a desperate place today, write a plea that you will be able to "feel" that hand encircling yours in comfort and strength.

Hold tightly to the One who loves you and stay close to Him.

Do not love this world
nor the things it offers you,
for when you love the world, you
do not have the love of the Father in you. For
the world offers only a craving for physical
pleasure, a craving for everything we see, and
pride in our achievements and possessions. These
are not from the Father, but are from this world.
And this world is fading away, along with
everything that people crave. But anyone who
does what pleases God will live forever.

–1 John 2:15-17

Turn from Worthless Things

Do not love this world nor the things it offers you, for when you love the world,
you do not have the love of the Father in you. For the world offers only a
craving for physical pleasure, a craving for everything we see, and pride in our
achievements and possessions. These are not from the Father, but are from this
world. And this world is fading away, along with everything that people crave.
But anyone who does what pleases God will live forever. —1 John 2:15-17

• • • • • • • • • • • • • • • • • •

I had a friend who was desperately unhappy. In terms of material possessions, she
appeared to have it all: wealth, a gorgeous home, ability to travel and visit exotic loca-
tions, a pretty face, a slender body—everything our world says brings happiness. But
no. She was miserable. She had literally two closets filled with clothing she had never
worn. Price tags still attached—the results of late-night shopping sprees online when
she couldn't sleep. She was haunted by life decisions she had made, and she continued
in patterns of destructive living that pushed her deeper and deeper into despair. Oh, how
my heart hurt for her!

From observing her pain, I learned a sobering lesson. "Stuff" does not bring happiness or joy or fulfillment. In the end, it's just inanimate matter that will fade and spoil
and lose its newness. And yet, how the world entices us! We're urged to buy more. We're
invited to live for pleasure. We're told we need the latest gadgets, we need to be the best,
to stand out in the crowd, to be the most successful . . . and all of that buying and doing
and attaining will bring us nothing but sorrow—if that is our focus.

To love the world and crave what the world offers, John says in the passage above, is
to walk away from the love of the Father! Jesus spoke very plainly when He said we cannot love both God and money: "No one can serve two masters. For you will hate one and
love the other; you will be devoted to one and despise the other. You cannot serve God
and be enslaved to money" (Luke 16:13). To love the world and crave all that the world
offers means investing in what fades away. No matter how rich we might find ourselves,
how popular we might be, how beautiful we might look . . . none of that will last. And it
grows pretty tedious after a while maintaining it all.

I want to live for what really matters, don't you? First and foremost, let's draw close to the God who made us, who fashioned us in our mothers' wombs with care and tenderness. Let's stay close to the One who is preparing a place for us, so that we can be with Him in great joy forever. And then let's invest in other human beings who also will have the opportunity to live forever in a place that defies description: Heaven. Paul encourages us in 1 Corinthians 2:9 that "eye has not seen, nor ear heard, nor have entered into the heart of man the things which God has prepared for those who love Him" (NKJV).

We have treasure awaiting us in Heaven beyond all imagining! Joy at being in the presence of Love Himself. Reunion with loved ones. Beauty beyond our ability to comprehend created by the same God who made our planet with snow-capped mountains and rivers and sunsets and grand vistas. We'll see shimmering rivers, trees of life, golden light, and life abundant that will never fade away or spoil. No pain. No sickness. No death. Can we live as if we believe this? What awaits us is so grand that all our hearts and our minds, our strength and our energy should be spent preparing—and striving to bring with us as many as we can!

Living in Him today . . . and knowing you have a future so amazing, so secure . . . will bring you joy, dear one. Joy with no regrets. Turn away from worthless things.

My Reflections

What are the "things" that trap you if you're not careful? Are you tempted by pretty stuff? By trying to always obtain or maintain the perfect body? Does seeking popularity threaten to come between God and you? Write out here your greatest temptation.

Read 1 Corinthians 10:13 and talk to God about your temptation, asking for His strength and His will for you.

Read 1 John 2:1-17. Choose a verse from this passage that resonates with you and write it out here.

Pray with me.

Heavenly Father, forgive me when I stray from You, my first love. Protect me from a world that whispers lies about the way to find satisfaction and peace. Free me from the traps of this world, designed to keep me craving what does not satisfy. Help me to walk away, unshackled and free to simply be Your child, loved and cared for abundantly. Thank You, Lord, for the sure hope of Heaven and for all the amazing and marvelous and permanent fulfillment that awaits me there. Help me to spend my energy and my life calling others to join me in this forever love You have for all who receive it! In Jesus' Name, Amen.

Smile. An amazing place is being prepared for you in Heaven.

Don't wait in ambush at
the home of the godly,
and don't raid the house
where the godly live.
The godly may trip seven times,
but they will get up again.
But one disaster is enough
to overthrow the wicked.

—Proverbs 24:15-16

Get Back Up

Don't wait in ambush at the home of the godly, and don't raid the house where the godly live. The godly may trip seven times, but they will get up again. But one disaster is enough to overthrow the wicked. —Proverbs 24:15-16

· · · · · · · · · · · · · · · ·

I remember stepping outside one freezing cold January day, happy as a lark, and then slipping on black ice. BAM! Down I went. And all that happy just flew away. Ouch! One moment I was full of energy and brightness and the next I was staring at the sky with a throbbing head. This was not fun. Not only was I hurt physically, but also the shock of it happening so suddenly took my breath away. I never saw it coming.

Life can be like that sometimes. Everything finally seems to be in order and then tragedy strikes without warning. A good day turns into a bad one in a nanosecond. Worse are the times when multiple hard unexpected circumstances hit all at once. In the middle of dealing with a handicapped parent, we are diagnosed with cancer. After an automobile accident, we're handed divorce papers. Bad things happen. Sometimes we're hit with a whole lot of them in a row until we are flat out on our backs stunned and helpless. It can be really, really hard to get back up in times like that.

That's why I love Proverbs 24:15-16. Yes, the houses of good people can be raided. Bad things can happen. Sometimes the "godly may trip seven times." Seven is symbolic in the Bible, but basically the writer of Proverbs is saying that bad things can happen over and over and over. But guess what? The godly . . . *will get up again.* They will not stay flattened forever. You know why? Because God is with them in the midst of it all. They are not alone. He will lift them up. He will also surround them with His Church—His hands and feet. Oh, friend, if you've been stunned by something hard, be reassured. He has not abandoned you. He will wrap you in His arms of love and see you through.

Sometimes what flattens us doesn't strike from the outside. Sometimes it's caused by our own sin and foolishness. Sadly, I cannot count the number of times I have wounded a friend or family member because of an out-of-control temper. My problems with anger go way back to tantrums as a young child. Over and over, although I wanted to do better, I found myself saying words I regretted and doing damage to my family and friends.

Like Paul, I've experienced times when ". . . I want to do what is right, but I can't. I want to do what is good, but I don't. I don't want to do what is wrong, but I do it anyway" (Romans 7:18b-19).

But even in times like that, because of the never-ending forgiveness of Christ, you and I can get back up. We can confess that sin . . . again. We can know that we are forgiven by the God who says to forgive seventy times seven times a day if needed (Matthew 18:22). So, if your particular problems stem from a sin in your life . . . never stop asking Him to forgive you. Just keep on confessing quickly and repentantly. He will forgive. He will not condemn. And someday, like me, you will find that the sin that seemed to be never-ending in your life will be vanquished by the power of the Holy Spirit.

That awful day I fell on the ice? It was still dark outside. No one was around to see me or to help me. And did I mention it was *cold*!? I needed to get up or get hypothermia. So . . . as much as it hurt, I managed to pick myself up. A nasty lump on my head stayed around for a while, but other than that, thank God, I was just fine. I'm very grateful that, despite the pain and shock, I was able to wobble back into the house. I thank God for His mercy on me that cold winter's day. God will help you, dear one, even when you're lying flat and hurt and helpless. It's stunning but true. He rescues you when the bad times come. And He forgives you over and over. Regardless of how you landed on your back, He will always lift you up again.

My Reflections

What's happening with you right now? Have you been hit by an unexpected tragedy or disaster? Are you struggling with a specific sin? Write it out and put it all down on paper before the Lord. Or if you are in a happy place right now, write that out here, rejoicing in this window of goodness God has given you.

Read Romans 7:15-8:4. Get a feel for this whole, tremendous passage. Paul goes from feeling defeated to remembering how Christ rescues him from the endless cycle of sin and guilt and shame. Isn't it a sweet section of Scripture? Write out your favorite verse.

Take some time talking to God about your day. Ask His help to see you through.

Whenever trouble comes, God is there to help you get back up.

Wounds
from a friend
can be trusted,
but an enemy
multiplies kisses.

—Proverbs 27:6

Find a Truth-Telling Friend

Wounds from a friend can be trusted, but an enemy
multiplies kisses. —Proverbs 27:6 NIV

• • • • • • • • • • • • • • • • •

"You don't look so good. You seem off," my friend said. "What's wrong?" Well, no one likes to be told they don't look good, now do they? Yet this comment was spoken in love and concern for my well-being. Any wounding that came from knowing I didn't look great that day was slight compared to the value of having a friend who truly saw me and wanted to help.

I've been blessed with excellent friends. They stop me if I start to gossip. They remind me to be grateful when I begin to sink into a self-pitying morass. When I sound bitter, they listen, of course, but they also gently point out the poison in my soul. These are women who know and love God, and I can trust them to speak truthfully to me for my own benefit. Because I know they love me, I can listen and learn from their counsel.

Trust me, I've had some unhelpful friends as well. The ones who entice me to gossip and who encourage me to think negatively about others. No matter how friendly they might seem, if they are critiquing others behind their backs . . . chances are good they're also critiquing me. It might feel nice in the moment to gripe about an unfair situation in my life and dump all the blame on someone other than myself, but in the end it leaves me worse and lessened.

Oh, my reader-friend, find a friend who will speak truth to you even if it wounds. Find a friend whose love for Jesus is evident in her life and conduct. Love her and be that friend to her also, both of you seeking a close walk with Christ above all else. Then, as "iron sharpens iron," pour truth and encouragement into each other's lives and, yes, the occasional wounding when needed. Pray together. Seek God when either of you is troubled. When the emotions start to swirl and bitterness or anger or envy rears an ugly head, turn it over to God through prayer, asking Him for a cleansed heart and a kinder attitude. This kind of friendship will enrich your life!

How do you find a friend like this? Begin by asking God to bring her into your life. Join a Bible study or a prayer group. Watch for ones in the group whose love for Jesus is contagious.

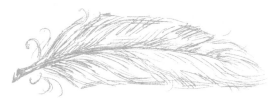

Ask Him to literally point out to you which woman He'd like you to get to know. Invite her over to your home or to a coffee shop and learn about her. And then, suggest that you share prayer requests and pray for each other right then. Or if you're in a public place and you feel more comfortable, wander out to your car and pray there. Nothing will cement a friendship better than two hearts joined together seeking God for His will for each other's lives and situations and families. Prayer is one of the best ways to form a deep relationship with a truth teller.

Back in my twenties, God brought such a woman into my life. She invited me to a prayer time with another friend of ours. During that first year together we added a fourth woman. We met weekly. We shared our lives over coffee and tea, honestly unloading the highs and the lows. But we always allowed at least half an hour for prayer, and truly it was prayer that mattered most. Each of us drew closer to the Lord—and to one another—because of those prayer times. Over forty years later, and living many miles apart, we original three are still praying for each other and sharing our hearts through email.

In every place our family has moved (and we've moved a lot!) I've asked God for at least one woman with whom I can pray. I'm smiling as I type, face after face appearing in my mind's eye, a parade of awesome women—each one unique—each one touched me at a time in my life by being there for prayer and counsel. May God bless you with a friend like these!

My Reflections

Read these proverbs on friendship and then write down what you learn from each one.

> A friend loves at all times, and a brother is born for a time of adversity.
> —Proverbs 17:17 NIV

> One who has unreliable friends soon comes to ruin, but there is a friend who sticks closer than a brother. —Proverbs 18:24 NIV

Do not forsake your friend or a friend of your family, and do not go to your relative's house when disaster strikes you — better a neighbor nearby than a relative far away. —Proverbs 27:10 NIV

As iron sharpens iron, so one person sharpens another. —Proverbs 27:17 NIV

Pray. If you need a praying, truth-telling friend, ask God for one. Otherwise, thank God for the friend or friends in your life who are faithful and true. And pray also that you will be that kind of friend.

May God bless you with a truth-telling, Jesus-loving friend!

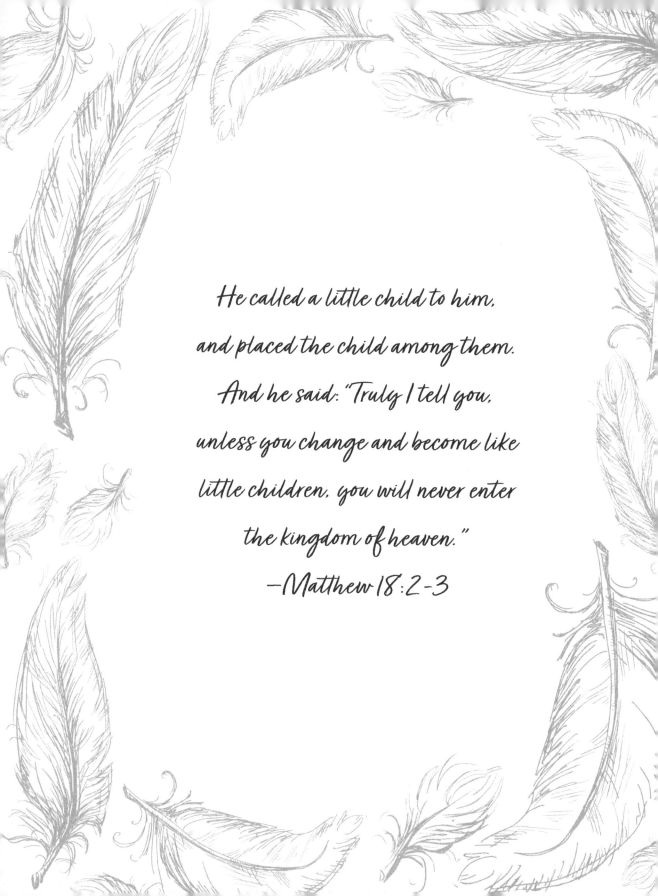

He called a little child to him,
and placed the child among them.
And he said: "Truly I tell you,
unless you change and become like
little children, you will never enter
the kingdom of heaven."
—Matthew 18:2-3

Dare to Ask

He called a little child to him, and placed the child among them. And he
said: "Truly I tell you, unless you change and become like little children,
you will never enter the kingdom of heaven." —Matthew 18:2-3 NIV

· · · · · · · · · · · · · · · · · ·

Let's talk about children. When they are quite small, their position is lowly indeed.
Completely dependent, they need help eating, dressing, even moving. If left all alone, a
human baby will die. That's pretty defenseless. We humans are born needy and require
someone to care for us. Even after a baby learns to talk and walk, the caring days are not
over. Now a child needs to be taught that electrical outlets are dangerous, that sitting in
a car without restraints means you could be severely injured in an accident or even die,
that a diet of sugar and fats will ruin the workings of your body over time—and countless
other life lessons.

Here's something they seem to know without any help from us at all: asking questions! Yup, young children ask questions. All. The. Time. Until their parents' heads are
swimming. And it's not my imagination. I came across this study online in Britain's news-
paper, *The Telegraph*.

Research shows mothers are the most quizzed people in the UK, and on subjects
far and wide. They are asked more questions every hour than a primary school
teacher—19—as well as doctors and nurses, 18. And the study discovered girls aged
four are the most curious, asking an incredible 390 questions per day—averaging a
question every 1 minute 56 seconds of their waking day. (March 28, 2018)

As I've pondered this "asking thing" a child does, I've learned a lot about asking
questions of my Heavenly Father. After all, I'm a child of the very best parent on the
planet. In fact, God is the only perfect parent on the planet!

I can ask God all the questions I want. It's natural and normal for a child to ask her
parent questions. Tons of them evidently. And unlike a human parent who might
weary of my questions . . . my Heavenly Father will never grow weary of my asking.

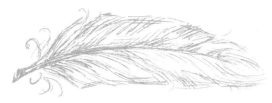

I can ask God trivial questions as well as deep ones. I don't have to worry if my questions make perfect sense or not. I don't have to phrase them like I would to a seminary professor. I'm a child. I can ask silly questions of my loving Father, any old way I want. He won't judge me . . . He knows I'm just a kid.

I can expect that He won't give me everything I ask for. What child has a parent who always says yes to them? Even super lenient parents won't agree to their child racing across a highway into heavy traffic. How much more will my good Father say no to questions I've asked or requests I've made that He knows will not bring about His best in my life—or in the world at large.

Just because God, my parent, says no to one request, doesn't mean I should never ask Him for anything again. What child walks away when their parent says no and never asks for anything else? Children keep asking, don't they? Jesus tells us to ask Him for anything. We can accept a no answer from God and yet go back again with another request, trusting that our good Father will answer wisely.

Approach God with the childlike faith He longs for you to have. Delight in being His kid with access to Him all the time for any question that is on your mind and with any request that is dear to your heart.

My Reflections

Read Matthew 7:7-12. What do you learn about God as a Father from this passage? What do you learn about asking questions of Him?

Reflect on your own childhood. Did you have parents who heard and answered you? Rejoice in that. Thank God for them, because they have made it easier for you to approach your Heavenly Father by their good example. However, if you had parents who were often arbitrary and unpredictable, ask God to help you see Him through a different lens. Remember that He is the good and perfect parent. Ask Him to help you trust Him in this. Write your prayer.

You are God's child. Go ahead. Ask Him.

Always be joyful.

Never stop praying.

Be thankful in all circumstances,

for this is God's will

for you who belong to Christ Jesus.

Do not stifle the Holy Spirit.

Do not scoff at prophecies,

but test everything that is said.

Hold on to what is good.

Stay away from every kind of evil.

—1 Thessalonians 5:16-22

Say Goodbye to the Pity Puddle

Always be joyful. Never stop praying. Be thankful in all circumstances, for this is God's will for you who belong to Christ Jesus. Do not stifle the Holy Spirit. Do not scoff at prophecies, but test everything that is said. Hold on to what is good. Stay away from every kind of evil. –1 Thessalonians 5:16-22

• • • • • • • • • • • • • • • • • •

I don't mind the occasional puddle on a rainy day. Normally, I can walk around it, and if I have my boots on and am feeling particularly juvenile, I can slosh right through it. However, when it has rained three weeks straight and the puddles have joined together to form some kind of perverse and mucky lake and you have to walk through them because there's no way around and the water pours in over your shoes and gushes your toes . . . well that's a different story. Yuck.

Imagine, though, if instead of slogging on through the huge puddle with water seeping into my shoes, I stop and sit down in it. And what if, instead of trudging through to the other side, I just gloomily sit there and splash dirty water over my entire body, even dribbling it over my head and face. Now that's a scary picture, isn't it? Who would do that? I mean, seriously only someone with a very disturbed mind, right?

And yet. At times, we can be guilty of that kind of wallowing in our thought lives. We hit a stretch when everything is going wrong. We don't just have a puddle or two of bad news . . . we have an enormous lake. And instead of moving on, asking God for strength, we kind of just sit down in it and make it worse by soaking ourselves in self-pity and dismay.

This will not help us get through life well. In fact, it's just as detrimental as sitting in an actual puddle. Don't do it. Get up, dear one, and slog through. It will end.

Paul gives advice to the Christians who lived in the city of Thessalonica. They were in the minority, and not everyone loved them in the city. In fact, Paul and his companions had to literally run for their lives. The church they left behind had it tough. Some were undoubtedly persecuted for their faith. They could easily have given in to self-pity and dismay. Notice what Paul tells them to do instead. They were to "Always be joyful. Never stop praying. Be thankful in all circumstances . . ." (1 Thessalonians 5:16-18a).

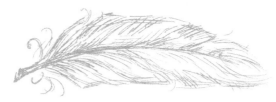

Even in the toughest of times, they were to keep going in their joy, in their prayers, and in their thanks. Why? Because God was with them through it all. They had been saved, were God's children, had the Holy Spirit indwelling them, and had a glorious future awaiting them in Heaven. God was going to do great things through them on earth. They just needed to keep going with Him.

We need to do the same. We can stifle the Holy Spirit through our ingratitude, our whining, and our self-focused angst. When we find the good even in the hard things, when we dare to say "thank You" to God for whatever purpose He has in the puddle He has allowed, when we don't stop praying no matter what . . . the joy comes! The Holy Spirit fills us with His joy. It's supernatural and crazy and totally true. We can be joyful in the worst of situations because of God's overwhelming Presence of Love with us. Oh, we need to hold on to what is good and think about that, fleeing from all evil thoughts and attitudes that would stunt us and keep us stuck. When your life is one big puddle, march on through it holding God's big hand and asking Him to help you notice the good in the midst of the hard. Hey, you might become so joy-filled you splash about a bit on your way to the other side!

My Reflections

Read Psalm 100 and write below every good thing to be grateful for in that psalm.

Write your own personal thank you list. Can you breathe? Do your legs work? Is there a roof over your head at night when you sleep? Do you have access to food and clean water? Oh my! If you answered yes to most or all of those questions, you have more than millions on this planet . . . you have much to write down, right here, that will remind you of the good in your life. May God use this list to help you "notice" your blessings!

My Thankful List:

Puddles don't last forever. And God is with you, dear one, even in the big ones.

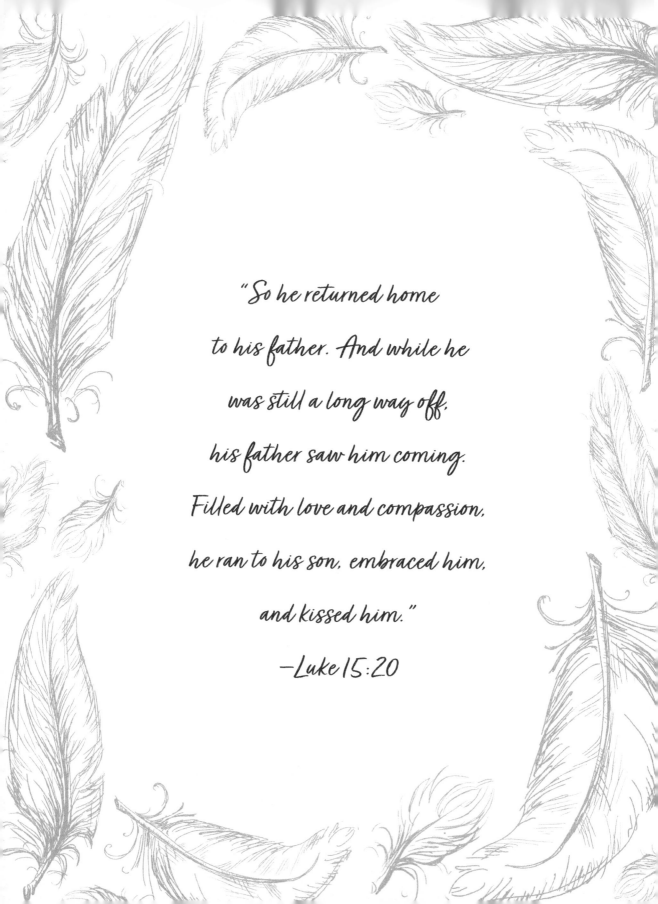

"So he returned home
to his father. And while he
was still a long way off,
his father saw him coming.
Filled with love and compassion,
he ran to his son, embraced him,
and kissed him."

—Luke 15:20

Risk the Hurt

"So he returned home to his father. And while he was still a long way
off, his father saw him coming. Filled with love and compassion, he
ran to his son, embraced him, and kissed him." —Luke 15:20

. . . .

Words hurt. Betrayal stings. Being misunderstood can feel like an unexpected blow to the gut. I've felt the pain and hurt that comes from the "slings and arrows" of others, haven't you? It can make you super shy about trusting them again. In fact, one of the main reasons people stop attending church is relational hurt. Yeah. There's a sting to that. Especially since you expect better from Christian brothers and sisters. That's hard to get over.

However, I'm here to implore you . . . ask God to help you get over it. Seriously. Satan, the enemy of our souls, loves to inflict collateral damage on us even after the main attack is over. What does that look like? Someone hurts us . . . big time . . . and we instinctively withdraw. The problem is that if we prolong our withdrawal long past the initial wounding, we inflict additional damage on ourselves. Oh, there has to be a better way! And there is—the much harder, much better way of love. Jesus taught us that to follow Him is to love our enemies, and the Bible is filled with stories that guide us.

The Prodigal Son – Luke 15:11-32

The prodigal son's father had been betrayed in the worst way. Not only had his son demanded his inheritance while his dad was still living . . . not only had his son left him and gone to a faraway country . . . but every hard-earned penny the dad had made, his son had squandered in foolish, reckless, immoral ways. Imagine how you would feel.

And yet. When that prodigal turned to come home, his father ran to meet him, hugged him, kissed him, welcomed him, and rejoiced without scolding, without a harsh word.

When I've been hurt badly, Lord, help me to respond like that father. When a loved one turns and repents and asks for forgiveness, help me not to lecture. Help me to forgive freely and lovingly, to be glad that they want to live rightly.

Judas' Betrayal – John 13:1-30

Jesus' last night of freedom before His arrest was a long, hard night. He knew what was coming. And one of those hardships would come from one of His own dear ones—a member of His inner circle of best friends—who was about to betray Him. Judas would profit from his betrayal of the One who had loved him and shown him God's love in a thousand ways. Jesus had invested in him. Judas had seen the miracles, the compassion, the purity of the Savior. And yet. He chose betrayal that would lead to Jesus' crucifixion. And still . . . beforehand, knowing exactly what Judas was planning, Jesus knelt and washed his feet. Jesus spoke of the hurt, spoke of the betrayal, so Judas knew that He knew. Jesus loved him to the end. Unbelievable.

Lord, when a friend has betrayed me, help me to treat him or her with love anyway. Give me Your compassionate heart. Help me not to let the betrayal turn me into a bitter, resentful woman. I want to be pure in my thoughts like You were with Judas. Only by Your grace, Lord!

Paul's Conversion – Acts 9:1-19

Before Paul met Christ, his name was Saul, and he was an enemy of the brand new Christian community, a mortal enemy. Paul had participated in the stoning death of Stephen, a member of the young church, and had obtained authority to arrest and throw other Christians into prison. He was intensely and actively hunting them down to destroy Christianity. And then. Jesus appeared to him in a blinding light. Once Paul met Christ, he was all in. Every ounce of that intensity was then redirected toward telling the world of his new King! As you can imagine, it was a bit difficult to convince the Christians about his change of heart. One dear man, Ananias, was told by God to meet with Paul, touch his eyes to heal the blindness from his encounter with Jesus, and welcome him into the faith community. Yikes! Ananias had to reach out to the enemy. Helping Paul meant risking arrest—risking his life. Ananias obeyed . . . reluctantly. But because he did, Paul was freed of blindness and enabled to serve Jesus with passion for the rest of his life.

Father, help us do the right thing. Help us to love. To forgive. Help us to give second chances, third chances, and fourth chances . . . even forty-second chances.

When the Christian church gets it right, joy and power in the fellowship are the result—and great rejoicing in Heaven! I want to be a part of that. Don't you?

My Reflections

Choose one of the three passages of Scripture we chatted about today and read it through —about the prodigal son, Judas' betrayal, or Paul's conversion. Write down a key verse from the passage you select that grips you in some way.

Write out the reasons this verse resonates with you and what you learned from the passage.

Do you have a current situation that needs to be resolved? Pray about it. Do you need to forgive? As hard as it can be, God requires us to forgive. Depending on the situation, we may or may not be able to have an ongoing relationship with the one we have forgiven. This can be hard to discern and might require counseling from someone who knows the Lord and knows your situation fully.

Risk the hurt. Love all over again.

Then he said to the crowd,
"If any of you wants to be my
follower, you must give up your own way,
take up your cross daily, and follow me.
If you try to hang on to your life, you will lose it.
But if you give up your life for my sake, you
will save it. And what do you benefit if you
gain the whole world but are yourself
lost or destroyed?"

–Luke 9:23-25

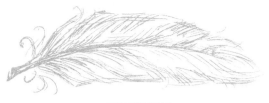

Take Up Your Cross

Then he said to the crowd, "If any of you wants to be my follower, you must give up your own way, take up your cross daily, and follow me. If you try to hang on to your life, you will lose it. But if you give up your life for my sake, you will save it. And what do you benefit if you gain the whole world but are yourself lost or destroyed?" —Luke 9:23-25

• • • • • • • • • • • • • • • • • •

Tucked inside my Bible is a picture of a Chinese Christian pastor who has been in prison for nine years. For some reason, when I saw the photo of him sitting in his study before his arrest, his wife smiling beside him, my heart was drawn to him and his plight. He looked so kind and comfortable, happy to be with his wife and at home with his books. When I imagined the different life he is now living in prison, being "re-educated," something in me just cried. So I printed that picture and put it in my Bible so that I would remember to pray for him, to pray that God would give him the strength to endure. God has given me new ways to pray for this man each day.

Not only is it a privilege to pray, it also reminds me of a sobering truth. We too must always be prepared to take up our cross for Christ's sake. Sitting here in my comfortable and slightly messy office, surrounded by my books and pictures of my family, it's hard for me to imagine being arrested and dragged away from all my comforts. But Jesus asks this hard thing of His followers: a daily willingness to lay aside our own will, embrace His will, and follow Him come what may.

Now, most of us will not be asked to give up our lives as Jesus did. Most of us will not be dragged away to prison or tortured. But that's the incredible commitment He asks of us. ". . . To be my follower, you must give up your own way, take up your cross daily, and follow me." He's quite clear: "If you try to hang on to your life, you will lose it." Daily, He asks us to lay down our own lives, our own plans, and stand ready to say yes to His will. That's the kind of all-in follower He desires—and that's the kind of follower He can use for His Kingdom.

Each new day we have a choice. Will we say yes to Him? Are we that sure of His calling and His love that we would literally follow Him anywhere? Truly, His question

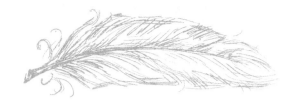

makes sense: "And what do you benefit if you gain the whole world but are yourself lost or destroyed?" His ways are best, dear one. As you have nestled in and learned how much He loves you . . . can you trust Him even with your life? The life that He actually gave you anyway? The greatest joy comes when we lay down our own agenda and choose the way of the cross.

Remember where the cross leads . . . to resurrection, eternal life, and a hope that does not disappoint. You can trust Him. Even with your very life.

Hanging on my wall is a prayer by a missionary who did lose her life for Christ. I read it often and it helps me stay in that place of surrender and willingness. Read these rich words with me as we close out our time in the Nest.

> *Lord, I give up all my own plans and purposes, all my own desires and hopes, and accept Thy will for my life. I give myself, my life, my all utterly to Thee to be Thine forever. Fill me and seal me with the Holy Spirit. Use me as Thou wilt. Send me where Thou wilt, and work out Thy whole will for my life at any cost now and forever.* (Betty Scott Stam, an American Christian missionary to China martyred for her faith in 1934)

My Reflections

Read Isaiah 43:1-13.

What does this teach you about God's presence in the midst of trials?

As you think about the Chinese pastor in prison that I mentioned in this devotional, how would these verses sustain him? How might they sustain you if you should be asked to literally lay down your life for Christ? How might they help you in your daily act of taking up the cross, willingly laying down your own way, and choosing His plans for the day?

Write a prayer, telling Jesus of your surrender or asking for His help in the days ahead to be able to take that step of trust.

Dare to choose surrender.

O God,

You are my God;

Early will I seek You; . . .

–Psalm 63:1a

Flight

Flight Lessons Introduction

O God, You are my God; Early will I seek You; . . . —Psalm 63:1a NKJV

• •

This morning was a typical one at our house. The coffee and tea were ready, a lunch was packed, and now I was sitting on the couch in my favorite spot with my Bible on my lap. I had just started getting comfortable when a flash of white fur zipped across the floor, leaped onto that lap barely giving me time to get my Bible out of the way. Yep. Miss Bella, my 13-pound, fluffy little white dog, had claimed her quiet time spot—my lap. With the Bible now perched on the arm of the couch, I continued reading while stroking a puppy, who was busy licking my hand.

I remembered back in time about 20 years ago sitting in the exact same spot with a pet on my lap—Tiger-Lily, our cat at the time. Other than the fact that she never licked my hand as I stroked her, the setting was pretty much identical. I smiled. Suddenly, I felt a warm, fuzzy sensation. Wow. I've been doing this sweet thing for a very long time—and I still absolutely love it. I believe God smiled too. After all, this is "our time."

It's difficult to find words to describe the joy that comes from consistently meeting with God every single day for decades. When I think about it day by day, it doesn't seem like a big deal—and the temptation to skip a day when I'm tired or grumpy is huge. However, committing to the big and irrevocable decision that meeting with God is more important than eating, drinking, going to work, or brushing my teeth (all certainly essentials) . . . has changed my life. Any good thing in me has been at least partially formed by the steady rhythm of my daily quiet times with God.

How I long for you to know this same joy! With all my heart. This book was written with the great desire of helping more individuals discover the life-changing lessons and fulfillment that come as we seek Him daily, as we grow to know Him more intimately.

You and I have been together for a little while now in our Nest lessons. Before a wee bird takes flight, it needs time in the nest to be nourished and to learn more about being a bird, right? Hopefully, your confidence in knowing God has grown as we have explored who you are in Christ. My hope is that you're now ready to flap your wings a bit and take some short flights, digging deeper into God's Word on your own.

The next four days will set the groundwork for the largest section of this devotional journey, Flight, as I introduce you to four key concepts that will guide you in studying God's Word, His love letter to you. Are you ready to teeter toward the edge and flap those wings of yours?

I love to share this four-step system of Bible study. I have found that it provides structure that allows me to approach my quiet time with enthusiasm and brings understanding and insight. Each step begins with the letter R: Request, Read, Record, Respond. I've been using this method for over 30 years, and I've never found it stale. Each time I meet with God using the 4Rs, the time is rich and fresh. We'll start with the first R tomorrow. For today let's reflect on Psalm 63.

My Reflections

Read Psalm 63.

Write a short prayer and talk to God about what you learned from this psalm.

Flight Lesson 1: Request - Learn to Ask

"Whoever humbles himself like this child is the greatest in
the kingdom of heaven." —Matthew 18:4 ESV

. . . .

Consider tiny children. They don't have much power or authority, do they? If they're hungry or thirsty, depending on their age, they either cry or shout or ask for something to eat or drink. They're completely reliant on others to provide all they need. Even when they ask or cry, they don't always get what they want. What if a child is intent on a game of some kind? If the person in charge decides it's naptime, then off he goes for a nap, hauled away from whatever-it-was that fascinated him and plunked down for much-needed, little-desired sleep.

Children are dependent. They aren't wise enough to grasp that vegetables are better for them than chocolate cake. They can't predict that missing a nap might turn them into an emotional basket case at dinnertime. Theirs is a humble position, ever needing someone to take care of them.

Jesus tells us that in order to enter His Kingdom we need to become like children. Whoa! This means we are to be humble. We are to acknowledge that we're not smart enough to have all the answers. When a great plan of ours falls through, we have to trust that the One in charge of us knows better. He sees the emotional basket cases we would become if He said yes to desires that would ultimately hurt us. Just like children, we are dependent and need to learn to make good choices of obedience and trust.

Each day as we begin our quiet time with God, the very first thing to remember is our position as His beloved child. Come to Him hungry and thirsty, longing to be filled with His goodness. And that is exactly what we ask. Request that He fill us as we read His Word. Oh, what an amazing difference it makes when we don't just open the Word and "grab anything out of it" like going to the refrigerator. If we stop and request help first . . . God shows us the best food—for us—that day.

Sometimes people are afraid to ask God for help. They fear: what if He's silent? What if He never answers? What if I'm left with a hollow feeling in the pit of my stomach wondering if maybe He isn't there at all? What if God doesn't grant what I ask? Will that

destroy my tenuous faith in Him? Oh, dear one, do not be afraid. Remember that little child who asks for food? Even if he doesn't get it, he asks again. And again. Kids don't walk away from a good parent the first time they are silent or the first time they say no. Not at all. Children aren't shy about requesting again, are they? Let's not be shy either! Before we read the Bible each day, let's request God's help.

Today's devotional and the next three devotionals will introduce you to the 4R Method: *Request, Read, Record, Respond*. For these four days I have completed the "Reflections" sections as examples of the kind of things you might write. Please use the space under "My Reflections" to record your own thoughts on each day's scriptures.

Sharon's Reflections

Request: *Father God, as I come to You to read a portion of Your Word will You please teach me? Open my eyes and ears, Lord, as I read. I want to learn. I want to hear from You. I ask this in the Name of Jesus, Amen.*

Read: Psalm 100

Record: I chose verse 1. "Make a joyful noise to the LORD, all the earth!"

Respond: My response is in the form of a prayer. *Oh, Lord, this verse makes me smile. Sometimes I really don't sound "pretty" at all. I'm just noisy. But You tell me it's okay to make a joyful noise to You. So I shout, You are my God, and I love being Yours! As I start my day, Lord, help me to remember whose I am. I'm so very grateful that You don't require me to be super talented or profound in order to belong to You. Amen.*

My Reflections

Ask for God's wisdom and insight. Then read Psalm 100 and share your thoughts. Don't hold back. You'll find plenty of space on the next page.

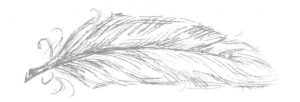

DAY 18 FLIGHT

Flight Lesson 2: Read – Choose Bible Reading

How sweet your words taste to me; they are sweeter than honey. Your commandments give me understanding; no wonder I hate every false way of life. Your word is a lamp to guide my feet and a light for my path. —Psalm 119:103-105

• • • • • • • • • • • • • • • • •

Do you have a favorite food or beverage you just love to eat or drink? Oh, I do—tea. I don't just like it. I love it. My mother is British, so maybe that's why I'm quite fussy about my tea and must have what I consider a proper cuppa. I'm talking strong, caffeinated black tea, brewed for at least three minutes with lots of milk. Now I fully realize that might not be everyone's "cup of tea." [Smile.] But it is mine!

I remember drinking tea as a tiny little girl. My mother called it "cambric" tea, which was basically a lot of milk with a bit of tea and sugar. I felt so grownup drinking my cup of tea with her. As we sipped together, I shared my little dreams and ideas with her, and she listened. When I grew older, tea became a comfort. When things were wrong in my life, a friend hurt my feelings, or I felt crushed, my mom would make us tea and listen as I poured out all my hurts. And when I hurt myself literally and needed bandaging of some sort, out would come the tea. So for me, tea is more than just a drink, it's an experience that evokes memories of comfort and being heard and valued. I love tea.

Our verses for today are from the longest chapter in the Bible, Psalm 119. This entire psalm is dedicated to the wisdom and joy found in reading God's Word. Seriously, the longest chapter in the Bible, and it's all about reading and learning and knowing God's Word. We are encouraged to love it more even than I love my tea. Let's take a deeper look at the reasons why from these three verses.

How sweet your words taste to me; they are sweeter than honey (vs. 103). Let's pause there for just a moment and figure out why the Word of God is so sweet. God . . . the only uncreated Being . . . the One who spoke and stars and galaxies flashed into existence . . . the One who fashioned human beings from the dust of the earth and breathed life into them . . . the One who created you and me uniquely and for a purpose . . . God wrote to us. No other book ever written can accurately proclaim that God is the author. Over and over in its pages we are told that, although men wrote down the words, God breathed

those words into their hearts and minds and supervised the writing. When I open the Bible, I open to read what God has to say to me. That is astounding. It is beyond sweet to realize that He, who did not need me and who lived in perfect Light and Love without me, chose to create me. Then, that He would reach out to fellowship with me. Way sweeter than a good cup of tea. Way, way sweeter.

Your commandments give me understanding; no wonder I hate every false way of life (vs. 104). Life is hard and often super confusing. Without guidance, how quickly I can get off track and walk down a "false way." I need to be often in God's Word. Like All The Time. I forget that "Love is patient, love is kind." (It's actually quite horrifying how often I forget when a family member irritates me or I'm stuck in traffic.) I don't know much about technology, but I do know this. Labs rely on precise instrumentation that requires regular recalibration; otherwise their tests or research will not yield accurate results. An international guideline sets standards so instruments can be regularly brought back into exact conformity. It's the same with our lives. We can so easily wander off the right path. We need to frequently read His commandments for they give us the understanding that helps us calibrate our lives and keeps us lined up with God's standards and His best for us.

Your word is a lamp to guide my feet and a light for my path (vs. 105). Oh, we do need a lamp for our feet and a light for our path, don't we? Life is full of twists and turns. So many attractive-looking side paths beckon us, but they are not the way we're meant to go. The Bible guides us, step by step, as we read. It's the most exciting book on the planet. Never stale. Never old. It speaks to us because it's written by God Himself. He moves in our hearts as we read, bringing freshness to verses we've read before, showing us how they fit our present pathway.

So . . . if we're going to take flight, let there be no substitutes. Let's not just read about God's Word. Let's open His Word and dig in. The *Read* step of our 4R Method is intended that we read with purpose. In fact, we will be looking as we read for "one verse" that especially stands out to us. Often that means we read the passage a couple of times. The first "read" is for context and the overall picture. The second "read" is to seek God for the verse that will light our path for that particular day. Are you ready? Again, I've recorded my reflections as an example. Space for your reflections follows.

Sharon's Reflections

Request: *Dear Lord, please give me a word today. Light my path as I read what You wrote for me. Help me to gain from it and to put into practice what You tell me as I read. Give me focus and an eagerness to hear from You. In Jesus' Name, Amen.*

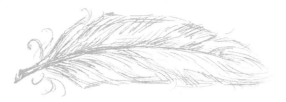

Read: Psalm 119:1-8

Record: I chose verse 1. "Joyful are people of integrity, who follow the instructions of the LORD."

Respond: *Oh, Father, how I love that following Your instructions leads to joy! You fill those who are in Your Word with great joy. We are happy. You don't write to condemn us or to make us ashamed. You write to teach us and enable us to live the lives You planned for us long ago. Thank You for the joy, Lord. Amen.*

My Reflections

Pray before you begin. Read Psalm 119:1-8 and share your thoughts.

Flight Lesson 3: Record – Notice His Words

Be strong and very courageous. Be careful to obey all the instructions Moses gave you. Do not deviate from them, turning either to the right or to the left. Then you will be successful in everything you do. Study this Book of Instruction continually. Meditate on it day and night so you will be sure to obey everything written in it. Only then will you prosper and succeed in all you do. This is my command—be strong and courageous! Do not be afraid or discouraged. For the LORD your God is with you wherever you go. —Joshua 1:7-9

• • • • • • • • • • • • • • • • • •

It's amazing how a woman can multitask. She can be scrolling through her phone while standing in line at the grocery store and still hear the conversation going on between the cashier and the customer in front of her. Yep. We're pretty amazing. At the same time, that amazingness can also be a real detriment. You see, we can also be reading the Bible (sort of) while planning out our next activity for the day, or if we're not careful, we can read through an entire passage of Scripture and not have a clue what we've read because we're fretting about a difficult conversation we need to have with our friend. [Sigh.] In truth, recent research has shown that multitasking reduces efficiency; it seems our brains were made to focus on one task at a time.

In addition, when we simply read a book or an article, we often remember very little of what we read even a day later. However, when we read actively, taking notes, our retention of the material increases exponentially. And we do want to remember what God says to us when we meet with Him each day. That's why we record a verse in our journal, highlighting one key thought that God has revealed in our reading. A ton of research has been done on the value of writing when we read in order to remember what we read. In just a brief search of the Internet, I came up with the following quotes:

The most effective note-taking skills involve active rather than passive learning. Active learning places the responsibility for learning on the learner. Research has found that, for learning to be effective, students need to be doing things with the material they are engaging with (reading, writing, discussing, solving problems). (World Economic Forum, *How Note Taking Can Improve Your Memory*, by Claire Brown)

It seems that writing anything down makes us remember it better. On the other hand, not writing things down is just asking to forget. It's a kind of mental Catch-22: the only way not to have to write things down is to write them down so you remember them well enough not to have written them down. Oy! (Life Hack, *Writing and Remembering: Why We Remember What We Write*, by Dustin Wax)

I've been practicing this method of consistently finding and recording a verse in my daily quiet times for over thirty years, and I've filled many journals with my discoveries. Because I determine to look for "my" verse for the day and seek diligently to see what God might be teaching me, I find something new, fresh, and current for my daily walk with Him every time I read God's Word! It's amazing what happens when we focus on His Word, taking time to really read it and not just skim through so we can move on to the next thing.

Today's verses from the book of Joshua are rich. We can be strong and courageous as we seek our instructions for each day of our lives. When we are meditating on His Word "day and night," God tells us that we will prosper and succeed in our Christian walk. Let's read to learn and grow and to hear the living God speak to us, and let's record what He tells us so we never forget it. This method helps bring God's Word into our day and makes it a part of our lives. Definitely *Record* your verse each day. This simple habit will yield a bountiful harvest of priceless guidance for your life—and joy in God and His Word.

Again, as we study today's passage, I've given my thoughts for you. Then, in the space following, record your insights and put this powerful tool into practice.

Sharon's Reflections

Request: *Father, forgive me when I read with no intention of retaining Your words or letting them penetrate deep. I want to truly hear from You. I long for a word from You that will direct my path this very day. Lord, teach me as I read, please. In Jesus' Name, Amen.*

Read: 2 Timothy 3:14-17.

Record: I chose, "God uses [Scripture] to prepare and equip his people to do every good work" (vs. 17).

Respond: *Help me to see Your Word this way, Lord—as a means for preparing and equipping me. I love that You have good work planned for me to do. Thank You for a life with purpose. Lord, use me. Show me the good works You have for me. Give me eyes to see and strength to do Your will. In Jesus' Name, Amen.*

My Reflections

Begin with prayer for God's guidance. Read 2 Timothy 3:14-17. Record the verse that stands out to you and share your thoughts.

Flight Lesson 4: Respond – Make It Personal

God has given each of you a gift from his great variety of spiritual gifts. Use them well to serve one another. Do you have the gift of speaking? Then speak as though God himself were speaking through you. Do you have the gift of helping others? Do it with all the strength and energy that God supplies. Then everything you do will bring glory to God through Jesus Christ. All glory and power to him forever and ever! Amen. —1 Peter 4:10-11

• • • • • • • • • • • • • • • • •

I was attending the annual Moms in Prayer Leadership Getaway in California. Serving as the New England regional director at the time, I loved those getaways. Oh, so much! Spending an entire week with women who love to pray. The joy, the kindness, the fellowship was rich and flowing. Life was going well. I was thankful for my relatively new position in the ministry, I loved praying for the New England region, and I loved the state coordinators in each of "my" states. In short, I was a pretty happy camper. (Although we weren't camping. We were at a Christian conference center. Literal camping might have been slightly less happy. I do like sleeping on an actual mattress with actual walls around me and a ceiling overhead.)

At the time, the ministry was without a national director, and in one session our team of regional directors was asked to pray about that need. We were urged to ask God . . . "is it me?" Well, I pretty much felt off the hook on this one. I was the most junior of the regional directors, and I loved what I was doing in New England. So, I prayed and asked, but I felt pretty confident that I would not be God's choice.

Then I opened my Bible for my daily quiet time. Here's the passage that was next in my readings:

Then Jesse told his son Abinadab to step forward and walk in front of Samuel. But Samuel said, "This is not the one the LORD has chosen." Next Jesse summoned Shimea, but Samuel said, "Neither is this the one the LORD has chosen." In the same way all seven of Jesse's sons were presented to Samuel. But Samuel said to Jesse, "The LORD has not chosen any of these." Then Samuel asked, "Are these all the sons you have?" "There is still the youngest," Jesse replied. "But he's out in the fields watching the sheep and goats. . . ." —1 Samuel 16:8-11a

Later that day, I just "happened" to read from the prayer of King Solomon in 1 Kings:

> "Now, O Lᴏʀᴅ my God, you have made me king instead of my father, David, but I am like a little child who doesn't know his way around. And here I am in the midst of your own chosen people, a nation so great and numerous they cannot be counted!"
> —1 Kings 3:7-8

Talk about a personal word from God to the "youngest" candidate for the position! But I couldn't announce myself as the next national director. How awkward. How presumptuous. How unlikely. I came before the Lord praying that He would confirm this call through someone else. As I was getting ready for bed that night, I heard a knock on my door. It was one of the other regional directors who had already been in bed when God nudged her to come over to my room and tell me what she'd felt all along—that I was His choice for national director. Wow! Confirmation indeed.

Why do I share this? Because it was such a marvel that God spoke so personally to me about His plans for me. God speaks to His people. And you, dear one, if you have accepted Christ as your Savior, are His people. You. Yes, you are. And as you read His Word every day, you will see how personally He speaks to you.

And when someone speaks to you, it's only polite to respond. When God reveals your verse for the day as you read, be sure you reply to Him, carefully and prayerfully, not rushing the moment. Converse with Him about the verse and His message to you. You truly do have a personal relationship with your Creator and the Lover of your soul. Respond to Him. He loves hearing from His child—like any good parent. That's why we always end our time in God's Word with a prayer response. We'll continue practicing that today as we study the selected passage. Remember, we're His kids. We don't have to sound like astute adults with multiple degrees after our names. We just share from our hearts in our own stumbly bumbly way. He wants to hear from you.

Sharon's Reflections

Request: *Lord God, open my heart to Your Word. Help me to come with an eagerness to learn and to hear from You. Speak, Lord. Your daughter is listening. In Christ's Name, Amen.*

Read: 1 Peter 4:7-11

Record: My verse is 1 Peter 4:9, "Cheerfully share your home with those who need a meal or a place to stay."

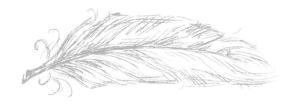

Respond: *Father, I'm stunned. Here I am in the middle of writing this book, and Ray and I are actually contemplating allowing someone to live with us for the next eight months. And here is This Verse right when I'm preparing This Lesson. Yes, Lord. Thy will be done. Enable us to welcome her with cheer, sharing our home with gladness, so grateful that we have an extra room evidently prepared for this young woman who needs it. Thank You, Lord, for Your personal and powerful Word. In Christ's Name, Amen.*

(So, that really just happened! We are praying about hosting a young woman who works with AmeriCorps. What do you think? I think God might just have given me His answer . . . wow.)

My Reflections

Request God's wisdom and insight in prayer. Read 1 Peter 4:7-11, and record the verse that speaks to you. Respond to God in a prayer.

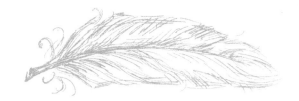

Now that you are familiar with the 4R Method, we will use all these tools and begin applying them tomorrow as we dive into a study of a book of the Bible. Here's a checklist as you prepare to take flight in your quiet time tomorrow:

    ❧ The time of day I will meet with God is _____

    ❧ The place I've chosen for our meetings is _____

    ❧ My Bible, journal, and pen are in place for easy access _____

    ❧ Steps I need to take in order to ensure this time happens are _____

_____

_____

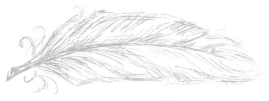

Daniel 1

Wait, what? The very first book of the Bible we're going to study using the 4R Method is . . . Daniel? But isn't that in the Old Testament? Really, really ancient? And doesn't it have some weird sections of prophecy? Won't it be too hard to understand?

Well, yes, we're starting with Daniel, and, yes, it may seem tricky, but it's a wonderful book of the Bible. One of my personal favorites. I actually picked Daniel because of its perceived difficulty. My goal is to show that you can study any book of the Bible for personal devotions. God tells us that "All Scripture is God-breathed and is useful for teaching, rebuking, correcting and training in righteousness, so that the servant of God may be thoroughly equipped for every good work" (2 Timothy 3:16-17 NIV).

Let's begin by asking the God who breathed this text into the mind of Daniel to speak to us through it. I believe He will answer that prayer. After all, He wants you to know Him and hear the stories of His love for His people. Every book of the Bible holds treasures for us and teaches us more about the One and Only King of kings who loves us. This one is an amazing tale of God's faithfulness to a man kidnapped and forced to serve in a foreign land.

Before we begin, you might consider reading about the book of Daniel and the background surrounding his story in your study Bible. You could also go online and check out what great Bible scholars and pastors have shared. I recommend Charles Swindoll's website, Insight for Living (insight.org/resources/bible/the-major-prophets/Daniel), but you will find many excellent sources.

I will not be providing a detailed background, because I'm not a biblical scholar with a Bible-related degree. I'm simply Sharon, a follower of Jesus, who believes that if I read this book—any book of the Bible—looking to God for His teaching, I will hear from Him. I also know that if I'm confused, I can go to the pastors at my church or to solid resources to help me understand. But for basic devotional reading of the Word, it's enough that I come with a heart eager to hear from God.

From this point on, we will begin with your reflections. My thoughts follow and are offered to you if you have time and interest. It is very important that you meet with God yourself first before reading my reflections. He speaks personally and directly to each one of us.

So . . . let's pray together and get started.

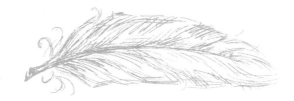

Dear Father God, as we begin this study of Daniel, a servant of Yours, will You please be our Teacher? Give us hearts that are open to You and minds that are focused as we read. We want to know You better and understand Your Word that was given to us because it is "useful for teaching, rebuking, correcting and training in righteousness, so that the servant of God may be thoroughly equipped for every good work." Please use this study in our lives to equip us. In Jesus' Name, Amen.

My Reflections

Use the prayer above or your own words asking God to reveal truth to you from His Word.

Request:

Read the passage through pondering what it must have been like to be ripped away from your family and your country, forced to learn foreign customs, a foreign religion, and a foreign language. Then forced into service of the king in this new land, the land that conquered yours. I can't begin to imagine what it must have felt like for these young men—all their dreams and plans completely upended.

Read: Daniel 1

Read the passage one more time and this time look for a verse that stands out to you. Maybe you'll choose one that's confusing or inspiring or a new thought to you. It's important then to write out the verse below. Simply choosing one isn't enough. Writing allows you to study it and remember it. I've discovered that when I slow down as I write, I gain deeper insight. God's words become more real.

Record:

Write a response to God about the verse you just recorded. Your thoughts don't have to be lengthy or super profound, but do reply to the God who just spoke to you!

Respond:

Sharon's Reflections

I'm always amazed when I read this book to think of the great loss Daniel and his friends suffered. Most commentators believe they even lost their ability to have children, because captives in service to the king were usually castrated. Isaiah had predicted this: "And some of your own sons, who will come from you, whom you will father, shall be taken away, and they shall be eunuchs in the palace of the king of Babylon" (Isaiah 39:7 ESV). How different this all seems from my world. I'm not a captive; I have family around me; and I'm female. Yet the culture in which I live has grown to have much in common with Babylon. Who knows what hard things God may ask me to endure? Reading about Daniel, I want to be mindful of the way this man reacted to adversity. How did he handle a life served up to him that was not of his choosing? *Teach me, Lord.*

Sharon's Verse: "To these four young men God gave knowledge and understanding of all kinds of literature and learning. And Daniel could understand visions and dreams of all kinds." —Daniel 1:17 NIV

Sharon's Response: *Lord, I love Daniel's humility as he wrote that You are the source of all that he and his friends knew and understood. He did not take credit for any of it. Not for his keen mind and not for his ability to understand visions and dreams. Forgive me, Lord, when I take credit for anything. I can do nothing unless You allow and enable it. You are my Creator. Help me to rejoice in Your gifts to me. I'm filled with awe at what You have done and are doing . . . all glory to You, Lord. Love, Sharon*

How I wish you and I could be sitting at a table with our cups of coffee or tea, sharing with each other the treasures God has shown us through the first chapter of this marvelous book. Did He surprise you? Are you going to "carry" in your mind the verse you chose today so that the thought God has given you stays with you and helps you? I hope so. See you back tomorrow for the next chapter. Have a blessed day walking beside the God who will never forsake you, even if you are suddenly captured and carried to a foreign land. Even then. He will be with you.

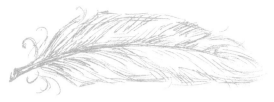

Daniel 2:1-23

As we prepare to read further in the book of Daniel, let's pause a minute and try to imagine what it must have been like to be the man Daniel. Most likely, he arrived in Babylon as a young teenager in the year 605 B.C. At the end of chapter one, we learn that Daniel served in Babylon until the first year of the reign of King Cyrus, which was 539 B.C. That is a span of 66 years. If he were 14 at the time of his capture, he would have been 80 at the end of his career. If he were an older teen, he'd have been even older.

What a life! Ripped from his home and his family and taken from his homeland. Probably castrated and not even allowed to keep his own name, but given a new one: Belteshazzar. I'm just about positive that Daniel would never have chosen this life for himself. Yet so often, life doesn't work out according to our plans. Our losses might not be as extreme as his were, but we all have losses. Unmet expectations are part of being human. We cannot control much of what happens to us—but with God's grace and help, we can control how we respond.

This is why I simply love Daniel. He consistently made wise choices while living a life he did not choose. I want to soak up every bit of learning I can about him as I go about living my own life. I want to be more like him, serving God faithfully, even when it sure seems God has not blessed me in the ways I think He should have.

Are you ready for chapter 2? Let's pray together before you begin.

Father God, thank You for the example Daniel sets of believing You, trusting You, and following You no matter what. Teach us, Lord, as we read more of his story. Show us the truths in this chapter that You want us to practice in our own lives. We yield our hearts and minds to You. In Jesus' Name, Amen.

My Reflections

Use the preceding prayer or your own words and invite God to show you what He has for you today.

Request:

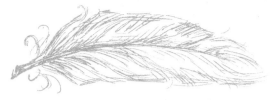

Remember to read through twice, looking for your verse on the second read-through.

Read: Daniel 2:1-23

Write out your verse. (Another friendly reminder that writing cements the words and thoughts in your mind far more effectively than just reading.)

Record:

Write a response to the Lord based on your verse and all He is teaching you.

Respond:

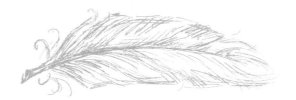

Sharon's Reflections

My thoughts are only to be read after you have written your own reflections. This book is all about meeting with God yourself, so no cheating! *Request, Read, Record,* and *Respond* first. Then if you have time, read my reflections.

Can you imagine the role of a wise man or magician in Nebuchadnezzar's court? You had to somehow know what on earth the king had dreamt? And then interpret it? Good grief! No wonder they were flummoxed. And yet, I think I understand why Nebuchadnezzar set it up that way. He was really and truly frightened by his dream. I suspect he knew it wasn't an ordinary one, and he was badly shaken. How could he possibly

know what the dream meant? Only if someone could tell him and that was pretty much impossible. Then could he truly trust the interpretation? He must have been desperate. Surely he knew that the most likely outcome was that all his wisest advisors would be killed. Not generally a great way to run a government!

And then, here comes our Daniel. Willing to go speak to this mad and crazy king who is asking the impossible. Actually being granted a little more time. But what Daniel does next is the reason he is such an amazing role model for us. He wastes no time worrying, but goes home, forms a prayer meeting, and seeks the Lord. He was calm enough that he actually slept that night, and while he slept, God gave him the answer. Wow. Another thing I love? After he wakes up, there's no bragging. He knows who has the answer to all mysteries, all knowledge, all wisdom. He praises God in a beautiful poetry prayer, giving glory to the One who did the impossible.

Think about it for a moment. Had God protected Daniel and his friends from the marauding Babylonians? No. As captives in a foreign land, it would be easy to understand if Daniel had decided the last place to go for help was to the God of Israel, the One who had allowed the capture of His people. But no, Daniel didn't perceive the situation that way. I suspect he knew full well why God had allowed the invasion. If he had read or heard the prophets or their warnings, he understood that Israel totally deserved punishment for her long history of idolatry. In fact, Daniel's very captivity underlined the trustworthiness of His God: God said He'd let His people be captured . . . and He did.

Sharon's Verse: "He controls the course of world events; he removes kings and sets up other kings. He gives wisdom to the wise and knowledge to the scholars." —Daniel 2:21

Sharon's Response: *Father God, this world can be a frightening place. I needed this reminder that You are in control of it all. You can take down any man or woman who is in authority at any time. They only have their current power because You have allowed it. In the end, they will bow their knee to You either in terror or reverence. This is a great comfort to me. I praise You and I thank You for the safety I feel knowing You are in control. In Jesus' Name, Amen.*

Isn't it amazing how much we can learn from God's living Word? I hope you are loving this study as much as I am. May God teach you more about who He is. "And this is the way to have eternal life—to know you, the only true God, and Jesus Christ, the one you sent to earth" (John 17:3).

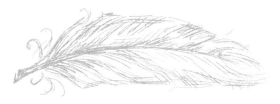

Daniel 2:24-49

I'm still amazed that Daniel was able to wait on the Lord for an answer throughout that long night before his possible execution. As I think about it more, I wonder if Daniel actually did sleep at all or whether the vision came to him while he was praying. In any case, as Daniel waited on the Lord, knowing that in his own wisdom he was helpless to fathom what another man had dreamed, God came and unfolded to Daniel the entire mystery.

Can you imagine? Daniel saw what Nebuchadnezzar had seen. God repeated the dream in every detail. This was no ordinary dream. God had a special message for the king of Babylon. And since the dream and interpretation are recorded in the Bible, the message is from God to us as well.

I want to be like Daniel. I want to run to God with the impossible and wait on Him for help! I want to trust that God will reveal to me all I need to know—and I want to rest in what He chooses to leave secret. Our God is good. Our God is sovereign. All He does is right. We can trust Him and lean on Him, and we can always, always run to Him day or night.

So . . . let's see what this dream was all about.

Heavenly Father, how great You are! You reveal secrets through dreams and visions. You answer impossible requests. As we read this passage, would You please give us understanding? Teach us what You would have us know about this dream, a dream that was so important You sent it to a king—and You sent him an interpreter. In Jesus' Name we come to You now, asking You to open our eyes. Amen.

My Reflections

Personalize the preceding prayer or use your own words.

Request:

Read the scripture. Then read it again, looking for the verse that stands out to you.

Read: Daniel 2:24-49

Write your verse here. As you write, reflect on each word and ponder.

Record:

Write a response to the Lord based on that verse.

Respond:

Sharon's Reflections

I wish we could be together to discuss this. I'd love to know which verse you chose. I'd love to wrestle with you over what God meant with this puzzling dream. But since that isn't possible, I'll share my thoughts with you and trust that God has given you insight today.

As I read the details of the dream, I tried to picture it in my mind, did you? First of all, I pictured the statue as huge. In my imagination, I craned my neck to see the head so far away and so high up. Gleaming with gold, inscrutable, and scary. Then my eyes traveled downward, noting the silver chest and arms, big and brawny, and the belly and thighs of bronze, terrifying in bulk and size, then the iron legs and the curious feet that were iron and

clay all mixed together. As if that were not frightening enough seeing this looming, terrifying, gigantic statue of a man, then comes the rock. And what a rock! Hurtled through the air with might and strength, more immense by far than the massive statue, and it hits the feet with such force that the entire monumental statue crumbles into dust.

And did you notice what came next? A wind blew even the dust away. Nothing was left of that which had seemed so solid and so mighty and so immovable. Nothing. All. Gone. And then the rock grew until it covered the earth. Wow! What a visual picture of all the kingdoms of man that look so powerful and so frightening and are basically nothing compared to the Rock—to God Himself—who is far greater and far stronger than anything or anyone else.

You know, this actually comforted me. I can be a bit terrified when I read about evil men in our world today. They "seem" to have such power and might. However, God is bigger still, and at His appointed time all kingdoms built by men and all dictators who deem themselves so mighty will be swept away—so thoroughly no trace of them will remain. All that will be left is the Kingdom of God—and that Kingdom will be great and good. Hallelujah!

Sharon's Verse: "And it is not because I am wiser than anyone else that I know the secret of your dream, but because God wants you to understand what was in your heart." —Daniel 2:30

Sharon's Response: *Father, I love so much about this. First, Daniel talks to the king with an amazing confidence for someone perhaps still in his teens, in any case very young. And he's lecturing the greatest king on earth about You, God! Second, Daniel in no way tries to make himself look amazing. He knows full well he was helpless in this matter. Helpless. You wanted Nebuchadnezzar to know these things, Lord, and so You told Daniel. Father, help me to be like him. Help me never to take credit when really all I know, and all I am, is because of Your creativity in making me and teaching me and using me for Your Kingdom. Lord, help me to point to You like Daniel did. All wisdom comes from You. All glory goes to You. Amen.*

How much we have to learn and glean as we look to the Holy Spirit to open our eyes to the truth in the Bible! I hope you're encouraged to point to Christ like Daniel did. I hope you're comforted as I was to know that nothing evil will last—evil will all come tumbling down. But Christ, the Solid Rock, will stand. Have a wonderful time living this out today!

DAY 24 FLIGHT

Daniel 3:1-18

When we left Daniel yesterday, the king was honoring him. Actually, it all looked a bit awkward to me. Nebuchadnezzar is a confused man. He's bowing before Daniel after the dream is explained and yet praising the one true God as well. Daniel must have been a bit perturbed by the attention given him. After all, he had been careful to tell King Nebuchadnezzar that it was all God's doing. The end result was rather amazing.

Our Daniel, the one ripped from his home and dragged away as a captive, is now appointed to a high position in the king's court. Given gifts. The people of Babylon are commanded to offer sacrifices and burn sweet incense before Daniel. He's been promoted to ruler over the province of Babylon. What a change! We shall watch and see that, although he now has wealth and power, the essence of who Daniel is does not change. Not at all. I love his story so much!

Let's also note that Daniel does not forget his friends. While he serves at court, his friends are given other duties of significance in the province. Daniel is not self-centered. He cares that his friends are protected and blessed as well. Instead of growing all puffed up with his new status, right away he asks a favor on their behalf. Oh, to be that unselfish! I'm learning a lot. How about you?

Dear Lord, help us right now to take our minds off our troubles and off ourselves. Help us to look at Your Word with eagerness. As we read, give us our assignment and our directions for the way You would have us live. In Jesus' Name, Amen.

My Reflections

Personalize the preceding prayer and add your own words.

Request:

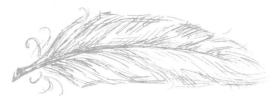

Read twice, carefully study, and learn about the passage as a whole. Then, ask God to show you one verse to focus on and ponder.

Read: Daniel 3:1-18

Write your verse in this space. (Sometimes I read the verse out loud as I write it, hearing the words as well as recording them. Try it.)

Record:

Write a response to the Lord based on that verse. Share with God all you are feeling and learning as you read.

Respond:

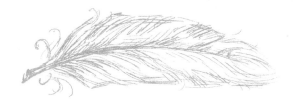

Sharon's Reflections

By this point, I'm quite sure you are doing your own study first. I suspect you have seen the value of reading and considering the Scriptures—just God and you together. My thoughts may add insight, and, of course, I hope they do, but what God shows you is most valuable for your walk with Him.

How fascinating that sometime after Nebuchadnezzar learns that his kingdom was the head of gold on the statue in his dream, he decides to build an entire statue out of gold.

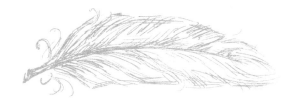

No silver kingdom following his, nor bronze or iron or clay! Just 90 towering feet of gold. Whoa. We're not seeing any humility here, are we? He may have temporarily praised Daniel's God, but he surely did not place his life under the God of gods. Nope. He was pretty proud.

In fact, it seems to me the height of pride to decide you need a 90-foot golden version of yourself erected and then order everyone to worship this statue, proclaiming that you are the greatest. And did you notice all the noise that went with the bowing? He had an entire orchestra out there next to the statue for crying out loud. Here are his people unable to go about their business earning a living, but commanded into hero-worship of him. I wonder how many men it took to melt enough gold for a 90-foot statue? How long did it take to shape it into the likeness of Nebuchadnezzar? How many people were out playing the horns, flutes, zithers, lyres, harps, pipes, and more?

And. How inconvenient. You're walking by the city square on your way to an appointment or hurrying home from work and all these zithers are making noise again. You have to suddenly drop whatever you are doing and fall on your face. Who cares about your schedule? Just bow when you're told because you and your life are of no value compared to this proud and silly king!

Oh, the foolishness of man!

Sharon's Verse: "Shadrach, Meshach, and Abednego replied, 'O Nebuchadnezzar, we do not need to defend ourselves before you.'" —Daniel 3:16

Sharon's Response: *Oh, Father! To be that confident in You! They spoke to the most powerful human on earth at that time and clearly told him that he wasn't the one they answered to. They answered to You. The King of kings. Help me answer to You, Lord, caring more about pleasing You than anyone here on earth! You alone. All honor. All glory. All praise. Amen.*

We sure have left Shadrach, Meshach, and Abednego in a rough spot. I confess to you that the thought of being burned to death is terrifying. The being dead part isn't what bothers me, because I wouldn't be. I'd be with Christ. It's the pain that comes first. It took a confident knowing that God is real and worth their whole lives to enable these three to refuse to bend the knee. Tomorrow, we'll see what happens next. In the meantime, go live for Christ today!

Daniel 3:19-30

You know one thing I really admire about Shadrach, Meshach, and Abednego from our reading yesterday? They acknowledged that, although they expected their God to deliver them from the fire, He might not. I see great wisdom in that. When we think we can "tell" God what to do because we know what's best, we're on shaky ground. God's ways are not our ways. I might think, for example, that the best thing for a friend's morale would be a promotion and pray for it with faith believing God will give it to her. And yet . . . God, who knows my friend far better than I do, might know that a promotion would lead to a stumbling block and temptation to sin. He may not grant my request, because He has her greater good in mind.

By acknowledging that God might not save them, Shadrach, Meshach, and Abednego keep God seated on the throne in their minds. He knows best. And yet, they also declare so wonderfully that no matter what God decides to do, He is still God and He is still good, and they were not about to bow to anyone else. Period. Oh, for a faith like that!

Now then, it's time to read what actually happened. Are you sitting in your favorite quiet time place? Or are you visiting somewhere and sitting in a hotel lobby or on a friend's couch? Wherever you are I hope you're curled up with a cup of something warm, eager to read God's Word and learn—but hold on to your seat. It's about to get hot.

Dear Lord, here we are, grateful for this time to know You better. Please open our hearts and minds to hear Your Voice. Despite any weariness, give us focus to really grasp what You would tell us from Your living Word. We love You, Lord, and we love being near You like this! In Jesus' Name, Amen.

My Reflections

Request:

Make sure you read through carefully and twice. Look for that verse you want to meditate on today.

Read: Daniel 3:19-30

Write your verse, pondering it with every word you write.

Record:

Write a response to the Lord based on your verse. Make it a prayer as you ask God for help in the day ahead and reflect on what He has shown you.

Respond:

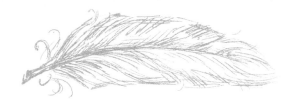

Sharon's Reflections

I have been pondering how Nebuchadnezzar could see into that furnace. Do you think it was open at the top so he could look down and see the four men walking around? Or was there a wide open door so the king could see the men being incinerated, the ones his fury had put there? How horrible that he wanted to watch! Yuck. I'm the kind of moviegoer who needs extremely family friendly movies. I hate viewing violence and cannot even imagine sitting down to watch people burn. Horrid!

It's fascinating how much detail is recorded as to the actual danger of the furnace. Daniel, who wrote this account, wanted us to be well aware that it would have been absolutely impossible for any human being to survive that kind of flame and heat. He shared

this in four distinct details. First, Nebuchadnezzar asked for it to be seven times hotter than normal. Second, the soldiers who threw Shadrach, Meshach, and Abednego into the furnace were themselves immediately caught up in the flames. Those poor men. Just doing their job. That's what rage does . . . hurts people. Nebuchadnezzar's anger-fit ended up killing good soldiers. [Sigh.] Third, these three friends of Daniel were bound, trussed up like three turkeys. They couldn't run or move. Fourth, they were still wearing all their clothes, which would presumably be very quickly consumed by flames. In short, no way on earth they could survive this punishment. None.

And yet. They did. They did! Wild and wonderful is this story! There they are walking around in the flames, clothing flapping about them, ropes that had bound them gone. And with them is this mysterious fourth man. What would it have been like to be thrown into a furnace and not be burned? To be with . . . an angel? . . . Jesus in a preincarnate appearance? Either way, feeling "peace that passes understanding" while searing hot flames do not burn them. My bet is they didn't want to come out when Nebuchadnezzar called them. Well, maybe they did. But still. Don't you want to talk with them in Heaven someday? Imagine what it must have been like to be rescued so totally and so dramatically. How they must have praised their great and mighty God! What a triumph this passage of Scripture is!

Sharon's Verse: "Nebuchadnezzar was so furious with Shadrach, Meshach, and Abednego that his face became distorted with rage. He commanded that the furnace be heated seven times hotter than usual." —Daniel 3:19

Sharon's Response: *Sadly, Father, I know that feeling of rage, when something I want is thwarted. What an awful, unholy act when a human being attempts to force his will on another at any cost. Thank You for calling me away from selfish anger and toward peace. I hate rage. It destroys and it's viciously selfish. Thank You that You forgive. Thank You for the fruit of Your Spirit that shows us a better way. How I want to walk in the Spirit today, Lord, and every day. Help me to live without rage. Fill me full with love, joy, peace, patience, kindness, goodness, faithfulness, gentleness, and self-control. In Jesus' Name, Amen.*

This passage left me breathless. What a wonder to read about God's amazing graciousness to these three young men who chose Him no matter what! Oh, let's live for Him! May God bless you as you hold onto Him, the mighty One, all day long.

Daniel 4:1-27

We find ourselves with a focus shift in our reading today. So far we've seen Daniel's world through his eyes and the eyes of his friends. We've looked at what it must have been like to live as captives in a strange and unholy culture. Perhaps we've found parallels with our own culture and have seen ways we also have to break from the crowd and the norms in order to hold true to what the Bible says. Today, we turn from the thoughts of captives with no freedom doing their best to stay true to their God and look at Babylon from the perspective of its ruler, who quite literally—from a human perspective—had it all. In fact, King Nebuchadnezzar himself wrote this chapter that became a part of our Bible.

King Nebuchadnezzar is a verifiable historical figure. Many historians over the centuries have attributed to Nebuchadnezzar the Hanging Gardens of Babylon, one of the seven wonders of the ancient world. He was definitely proud, making sure his name was inscribed on most of the bricks that were used to build the city of Babylon. In a simple Google search, I found various histories of this king and the overwhelming opinion of all—he was truly at the center of the world in his time, large and in charge!

In the book of Daniel, we see an intimate picture of King Nebuchadnezzar. Remember, Daniel was one of the king's closest advisors who worked with him and knew him well. The account of this king you are going to read today and tomorrow is incredible. As you read, marvel that God is greater than the greatest kings on earth and able to reach out to any one of them whenever He wishes. God so loved the world—and I see in this chapter God's love for Nebuchadnezzar. I'm inspired to pray for today's world leaders. They're not beyond the influence of our mighty God. Ever.

So . . . are you ready to read a bit more about Nebuchadnezzar? No fiery furnaces today. Just a sober warning and a harsh reality.

Heavenly Father, help us as we read Your Word to hear Your voice. Teach us through this ancient passage, and may it be a "living word" for us. Help us to learn much through Nebuchadnezzar's life and show us how to apply what we learn to our own lives. We ask this in the mighty Name of Jesus, Amen.

My Reflections

Request:

You may find it a bit harder some days to find a verse. However, I believe God will lead you to one that intrigues you or moves you in some way. Keep your eyes open for it as you read.

Read: Daniel 4:1-27

Write down your verse. Take time to meditate on it as you write it out.

Record:

Remember, your response can be a question, a matter of confusion you need help with—or a prayer of gratitude. Just speak for a while with the One who loves you and write down what He shows you.

Respond:

Sharon's Reflections

How would you feel if you were in Daniel's shoes and had to tell the king that God was going to take his mind away? No one likes the bearer of bad news. And Daniel was quite legitimately disturbed when he realized what Nebuchadnezzar's dream meant. By reading this passage and pondering it, I found a great deal of instruction for those times when we need to have a difficult conversation with someone. Here's what I learned, and I pray that God will use these principles in your life—and mine—and help us put them into practice the next time we have this unpleasant duty.

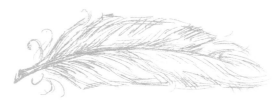

Daniel told the truth. I usually want to please people too much, which can make me slide away from speaking hard truths. I wince and cringe when I have to share something with a friend that I know she won't like. Years ago, a friend wrote to tell me about her new boyfriend. It was obvious from her letter that she was living with him. She was a believer, and the Bible is really clear about keeping oneself sexually pure before marriage. Trying to write to her out of my love for her and share my concerns about her choices and my desire that she follow Christ was very painful. Have you ever been in that place? We can learn a lot from Daniel. He told the king the whole truth. He told it clearly. He didn't shy away from it.

Daniel began sharing hard truth with honest love. His love for the king came shining through. He was visibly shaken. "Upon hearing this, Daniel . . . was overcome for a time, frightened by the meaning of the dream . . ." (Daniel 4:19a). He came to King Nebuchadnezzar emotionally shaken by what he'd have to say. Like Daniel, I need to be willing to ache for a friend or family member when I have to share a painful truth. There should be no arrogance in me and no legalistic pride. It should hurt to have to share something hard.

Daniel expressed his agony first. He writes, ". . . I wish the events foreshadowed in this dream would happen to your enemies, my lord, and not to you!" (Daniel 4:19b). People will be able to hear us so much better once they are assured that we love them and that our motive in speaking truth is a deep love for them—and for the God who loves them even more.

Daniel followed up his truth telling with a plea. He urged the king to repent and be saved from his folly. And he asked in humility with great respect. "King Nebuchadnezzar, please accept my advice. . . . Perhaps then you will continue to prosper" (Daniel 4:27).

Sharon's Verse: "King Nebuchadnezzar, please accept my advice. Stop sinning and do what is right. Break from your wicked past and be merciful to the poor. Perhaps then you will continue to prosper." —Daniel 4:27

Sharon's Response: *Lord, I'm struck by Daniel's kindness and love for this ruler. He manages to speak a harsh truth with love. Daniel knows You and Your mercy and believes that with a humbled heart his king might escape the fate of insanity. Help me to speak truth like Daniel, Lord, and help me to hold on to the sure knowing that You are merciful. In Jesus' Name, Amen.*

See you here tomorrow as we read what actually does happen to King Nebuchadnezzar. In the meantime, may God help you speak truth in love and grace.

Daniel 4:28-37

Let's do a quick checkup this morning before we begin. Since you are now in Flight, no longer in the Nest, and pondering the very words of God, how are you doing? Are you settling into a pattern and rhythm of time and place to meet with God? I hope so. If not, don't give up! Having this special time with Him each day is a privilege and honor. This mission to establish a pattern of daily time with Him is worth it, worth it, worth it! I'm very thankful you're here right now ready to read and study and seek His will for your life.

When we left King Nebuchadnezzar, he was greatly disturbed by another dream. I find it odd, considering his previous experience, that this king would waste valuable time calling in all the "wise men" of Babylon who had been completely helpless to interpret his previous dream. Hello? Daniel had proved to be rock solid at this dream interpretation thing—not only discerning the meaning of the dream, but even able to repeat exactly what the king had dreamed. Finally, the king sent for Daniel who once again by God's enabling explained the meaning of the dream. And now Nebuchadnezzar had a choice to make.

Because Daniel knew the mercy of God he pleaded with King Nebuchadnezzar to change his ways before it was too late. Based on his previous dealings with the God of Israel (let's not forget what happened in that fiery furnace), you would think King Nebuchadnezzar would listen, wouldn't you? But before we're too hard on him, let's remember how slow we can be to listen to the Lord. I know full well God wants me to be selfless and kind. I really do. Yet, I can still want to be first in line at the grocery store. I still look at a group photo and judge it based on how nice I look. [Sigh.] So, let's give King Nebuchadnezzar some grace as we read what happens next.

Open your Bible. Thank God for this precious bit of special time in His presence. Let's pray.

Oh, Father, please forgive us when we're slow to listen to You. Help us as we study and learn from Your Word. Give us eyes to see and ears to hear. Show us the path we should take this very day. We want to walk with You, Lord! We ask in Jesus' Name, Amen.

My Reflections

Request:

Ask God to show you "your" verse for the day as you read.

Read: Daniel 4:28-37

Write out your verse and ponder as you write.

Record:

Write a response to the Lord. Be honest and real with Him. Pour out your heart to Him if that is your need today. Our God is a loving and merciful God who longs to show you His love. He is the good Abba-Father you can trust.

Respond:

Sharon's Reflections

Well, King Nebuchadnezzar blew his chance. It's interesting that the demise of his mind happened 12 months later. I wonder . . . did he make an attempt at reform for a little while and then relaxed when nothing happened? Without the Holy Spirit and Christ's saving grace within him, it would actually have been impossible for him to "be good" indefinitely. Sadly, what finally did him in was his complete disregard for the God who made him and who empowered him and gave him that fine mind to begin with. He claimed that he alone had built that majestic city, that he alone was responsible for the greatness of Babylon.

And then he fell. From power and might and respect and homage . . . to total insanity, wandering, shuffling in the field with the animals, eating grass. What a miserable and troubling picture! It is remarkable to note that before Nebuchadnezzar was born, God

inspired the prophet Isaiah to write about this very incident. "How you are fallen from heaven, O shining star, son of the morning! . . . For you said to yourself, 'I will ascend to heaven and set my throne above God's stars.' . . . Instead, you will be brought down to the place of the dead, down to its lowest depths" (Isaiah 14:12a; 13a; 15). Lucifer also fell for a similar sin. Pride is a killer. God will not stand for us claiming that we are gods. He won't let us lie like that. Here are three verses that definitely underline the dangers of thinking we are fine in our own strength and merit. Note the consistency of the Bible as you read. This is a repeated message and one we should listen to with great respect.

> Pride goes before destruction and haughtiness before a fall. —Proverbs 16:18

> So anyone who becomes as humble as this little child is the greatest in the Kingdom of Heaven. —Matthew 18:4

> Humble yourselves before the Lord, and he will lift you up in honor. —James 4:10

Sharon's Verse: "All the people of the earth are nothing compared to Him. He does as He pleases among the angels of heaven and among the people of the earth. No one can stop Him or say to Him, 'What do you mean by doing these things?'" —Daniel 4:35

Sharon's Response: *This is the writing of a humbled man. He fully acknowledges, Lord, that You are the Most High. You are in charge and no one can change that irrefutable truth. How I praise You! The very fact that You are unchanging and unbeatable makes me feel so very safe with You. If You are for me as my Abba, I have nothing and no one to fear. Thank You, Jesus, for saving me and making me Your own! In Your name I pray, Amen.*

I've been quite sobered by what happened to King Nebuchadnezzar. I want to practice gratitude and remember that all I have and all I am are only because of God's gracious gifts to me. I don't want to boast about anything other than that I am His.

> This is what the LORD says: "Don't let the wise boast in their wisdom, or the powerful boast in their power, or the rich boast in their riches. But those who wish to boast should boast in this alone: that they truly know me and understand that I am the LORD who demonstrates unfailing love and who brings justice and righteousness to the earth, and that I delight in these things. I, the LORD, have spoken!" —Jeremiah 9:23-24

Psalm 1

Surprise! We're looking at a psalm today. For seven days we've been immersed in the book of Daniel, studying this bold and brave young man and watching the way he and his friends faced many trials. We've learned better how to deal with difficult situations. In a couple of days we'll be back with Daniel.

In the rest of this book, we're creating a rhythm for our study: every seven days we'll step away from our deep dive into the current study to spend a day in Psalms and a day in Proverbs. These two days will give us an opportunity to experience God's Word in two of the poetry/wisdom books of the Bible.

The book of Psalms is basically a songbook. Each of these magnificent psalms was written to be sung. It is by singing them that the meaning of the poetic words sinks deep into the hearts of the singers. Do you still have lyrics in your head from songs you sang as a teen? I do. Even though I didn't set out to memorize them, the repetition of singing along with a song over and over created a memory in my brain. So it is with the psalms. Set to music, these truths, these thoughts, these laments, and these praises *stick* in the minds of those who sing them. These are truths worthy of memorizing. Oh, I am so glad we're going to stop once in a while and explore a psalm!

Today's psalm actually fits in with our study of Daniel. It's all about making the right choices, helping us see what a good choice looks like, and showing the results of a life spent wisely, contrasted against the results of a life spent foolishly.

Let's pray and dig in.

Heavenly Father, as we turn to the book of Psalms, please teach us. We want to learn from You, dear Lord, how better to live out a life that pleases You. In Jesus' Name, Amen.

My Reflections

Request:

Ask God to show you "your" verse for the day.

Read: Psalm 1

Write your verse, and if you're the musical type, maybe try singing it as you write in your own made-up melody.

Record:

Why did you choose this verse? How can you apply it to your life? Take a moment to respond about "your" verse to the Lord who loves you.

Respond:

Sharon's Reflections

I love the imagery in Psalm 1. What a contrast between a tree and chaff! Think about it for a moment. A tree is big. Chaff is tiny. A tree can stand alone. Chaff is often found all clumped together. A tree is sturdy. Chaff is easily crushed. A tree lives for hundreds of years. Chaff does not. When the winds blow, a tree's roots keep it steady. It may sway, but remains immovable from its rooted place. When the winds blow, chaff has no control over itself. It goes where it's blown. It lands wherever the wind takes it. A tree is living. It drinks in water and grows each year. Chaff is dead. It can neither drink nor grow. A tree shelters other life. Squirrels and birds make homes in its branches. Human beings and animals find shelter under its leaves and shade from the heat of the day. Chaff helps no one and no one needs it.

In conclusion: I want to be a tree! I want to still be standing where I'm planted as God's child no matter what winds seek to blow me over. I want to drink deeply from the Word of God, filling myself with the "bread of life" and "living water" so that I grow in faith. I want to be shelter in a storm to those in need, harboring them and teaching them to drink water and grow roots in the soil of God's good Word. The thought of being blown about by every new fad or diet or political position makes me cringe. I don't want to be so mindless as to be taken in by what "everybody thinks." I want to anchor my life in Truth and stay there. How about you?

Sharon's Verse: "But not the wicked! They are like worthless chaff, scattered by the wind." —Psalm 1:4

Sharon's Response: *Father God, the contrast is so big! While trees stand straight and still, chaff is moved by the slightest breeze. Chaff is associated with a crowd—a lot of it and all flimsy. While trees have substance, chaff does not. I don't want to be a mindless part of a crowd blown here and there by the latest fad or belief. Make me a tree. Planted. Unique. Growing straight and tall. Nourished by Your loving Word! In Your Name and for Your glory, Amen.*

I wonder what Psalm 1 sounded like when it was sung. Do you think it was a catchy tune? I wonder if the part about the tree was "happy" and the part about the chaff was "darker" music. I wonder how many of God's people memorized that song and hummed it as they worked, letting the words sink deep into their minds. How I hope as we study God's Word, His truth will sink deep into our minds! Dig your roots deep into the soil of His Word. Be a tree, friend. Be a tree.

Proverbs 1

Today, we turn from Psalms to the book of Proverbs. The psalms were sung. The proverbs—pithy little sayings full of insight and easy to remember—were quoted. King Solomon wrote many of the proverbs found in the book of Proverbs, and he collected many more. The wisdom of Proverbs stands tried and true over the centuries, and we gain much instruction and save ourselves much grief when we listen to and obey their direction. Yet, keep in mind, a proverb is not a promise. A proverb tells us what will likely happen if we follow its direction, but God in His sovereignty allows trouble into our lives, and we live in a broken world. When a proverb teaches, for example, that if we save little by little we will one day be wealthy, God may overrule in our case. He may choose to allow hardships that keep us poor. But the principles found in the proverbs are full of truth and wisdom. A wise person will meditate upon them and ask for God's help in following their guidance.

The seventh verse of the first chapter of Proverbs is the theme for the whole book, the solid basis on which all the rest is built, "Fear of the LORD is the foundation of true knowledge, but fools despise wisdom and discipline." We need to start any quest for wisdom with the "fear of the Lord" as our foundation. What does it mean to fear Him? *The New Spirit-Filled Life Bible* puts it this way, "The fear of the LORD . . . is not the terror of a tyrant, but the kind of awe and respect which will lead to obedience to Him who is the wisest of all" (Proverbs 1:7). Charles Swindoll writes that the "fear of the Lord refers to the posture of reverence, worship, and respect that we ought to have toward God. It means living our lives in light of what we know of Him, holding Him in the highest estimation, and depending on Him with humble trust" (from *The Swindoll Study Bible NLT*).

Once we have placed God at the highest place in our minds and hearts, we can truly begin to learn and gain knowledge. Without God at the foundation, acknowledged as the Almighty, there can be no wisdom. We have to get the most important thing right. And the most important point is this: God exists and He is the author and creator of everything in the universe. So we start right there. Let's not be "fools" who "despise wisdom and discipline." Let's come to His book in humility, eager to learn from our Creator how to live wisely. Are you ready? Let's pray and dig in.

Dear Holy and Almighty God, we begin our time with You acknowledging Your rightful place as King of all. You hold all wisdom in Your hand. You are the Source of all knowledge. You made us and You know us, and we trust that Your guidance through Your Word is true and right and best for our lives. Help us to read in humility reverencing You and seeking Your truths for this day. In Jesus' Name, Amen.

My Reflections

Request:

Seek out the one verse you want to ponder and learn.

Read: Proverbs 1

Write out your verse, thinking about each word as you write.

Record:

Write your response to your God and Savior.

Respond:

Sharon's Reflections

Let's talk about Solomon, the writer of most of the Proverbs and certainly the writer of Proverbs 1. Solomon was well qualified to write this book. He had a rough beginning as the child of Bathsheba, a woman whose name is associated with scandal and disgrace. Her first child had died, born from an adulterous liaison with King David. I suspect her grief was intense and agonized as she wept for her little baby and all she had lost. Solomon was her second child—and an incredible object lesson of God's grace toward sinners.

For Solomon was declared by God to be the successor to David's throne ahead of older sons born from more conventional marriages. Solomon. The child of Bathsheba.

In 1 Kings 3:7-9, we learn more about this man when we read his humble prayer upon his succession to the throne. God tells the new king that He will give him whatever he desires and here is Solomon's response: "Now, O LORD my God, you have made me king instead of my father, David, but I am like a little child who doesn't know his way around. And here I am in the midst of your own chosen people, a nation so great and numerous they cannot be counted! Give me an understanding heart so that I can govern your people well and know the difference between right and wrong. For who by himself is able to govern this great people of yours?"

God granted Solomon's request, "I will give you what you asked for! I will give you a wise and understanding heart such as no one else has had or ever will have!" (1 Kings 3:12). Although Solomon made foolish choices and was led astray later in life by unbelieving wives, he still possessed the greatest wisdom a man has ever been given. Note, however, that *knowing* the right thing is not the same as *doing* the right thing. Our Solomon knew God's way, but erred because of sin. His last book, Ecclesiastes, is a telling indictment on the wasted parts of his life and yet it also brings hope, because in the end Solomon knew that the fear of the Lord really is the beginning of all wisdom.

Sharon's Verse: "My child, don't go along with them! Stay far away from their paths." — Proverbs 1:15

Sharon's Response: *Father, I'm so thankful for the lesson in this verse. We are not to see how close we can come to wickedness. We're to "stay far away." Peer pressure is a powerful thing, and once we start being buddies with individuals intent on evil, it can be way too easy to "go along." Lord, keep me far from those who would entice me toward evil. Help me to stay far from those dangerous paths. Keep me close to You. In Jesus' Name, Amen.*

As we turn back to Daniel tomorrow, let's consider what a wise man he was. He did not walk in paths of evil. Even in what "seemed" so benign as not following a Jewish diet in the Babylonian courts could have been a trap for him. He did not compromise back in those early days of his captivity. And that, dear one, is how to "be a tree" as we talked about yesterday in Psalm 1. Daniel "feared the Lord" and, because of that, he was a wise man in a hard place. I'm looking forward to getting back to his story. I'm glad, though, that we took a Psalm and Proverbs break these last two days. I've learned a lot.

Daniel 5:1-17

Today, we return to the study of Daniel, an amazing follower of the Most High God. If ever a man planted himself and studied Scripture and grew to be like a "tree" as we studied in Psalm 1, it was Daniel. If ever a man followed the directions of Proverbs 1 and made the "fear of the LORD the beginning of wisdom," it was Daniel. In fact, when God cries for Israel to turn from sin in Ezekiel 14, He speaks of Daniel. God declares three men righteous, and one of them is Daniel, "Even if Noah, Daniel, and Job were there, their righteousness would save no one but themselves, says the Sovereign LORD" (vs. 14).

Time has passed since we left Daniel. Nebuchadnezzar is no longer king, and the current king, Belshazzar, is at least two generations removed. Daniel is no longer a prominent advisor. In fact, he is unknown to this new king. I wonder what happened? Did Nebuchadnezzar's son promote his own advisors and demote his dad's advisors? Did Daniel simply retire at some point? It's clear, as you will see when you read this passage, that Nebuchadnezzar's successor has no respect for either Daniel or Daniel's God—our God. It's a sad story of drunkenness and wantonness.

To give some historical context, while Belshazzar is partying with his cronies, the city of Babylon is under siege. Belshazzar believes Babylon is invincible, and he isn't even worried that he will be defeated. What he didn't know that fateful night was that the Medes and Persians were secretly draining water from the river that flowed out of the city and redirecting it. This enabled them to creep into the city in the dried riverbed and attack from within. How foolish Belshazzar was! How foolish we all can be when we ignore an enemy and think we are invincible. I don't know about you, but I want to cling to God's big hand and stay close to Him as my refuge. No drunken partying, thank you. That leads to headaches, vomiting, and huge regrets, as you are about to see as you read the first part of Daniel 5.

Father, how we desire to stay close to You! Keep us from foolish decisions. Help us stay aware that the enemy of our souls wants to disrupt our fellowship with You. We choose to always abide close to Your side, Oh, great God! As we read this passage, teach us how to live well with You as our guide. In Jesus' Name, Amen.

My Reflections

Request:

Ask God to show you "your" verse for the day as you read.

Read: Daniel 5:1-17

Write out your verse and ponder as you write.

Record:

How are you doing with the "response" part of this method of study? I hope that, more and more, you are able to pour out your heart to the Lord in a written prayer, responding to Him about the Word you have just read. Write to Him now about the verse you have chosen.

Respond:

Sharon's Reflections

Belshazzar pretty much plumbed the depths of depravity and foolishness, didn't he? It wasn't enough that he threw a huge feast for over 1,000 people while his city was under siege. That would be tasteless enough in light of the suffering the poorer members of the city would be experiencing, unable to enter or leave the city and without supplies. No, Belshazzar decided to take the sacred cups from the treasury that came from the temple in Israel and drink out of them while toasting other gods—and not the One for whom the goblets had been made. Now that's not only tasteless, that's reckless and risky!

I doubt that anything less than a supernatural, totally spooky hand detached from a body could have shaken him. No human messenger would have dented Belshazzar's foolish sense of invincibility. If the hand had just hovered a while and left, he may have

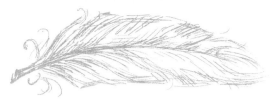

shaken it off as "not real." But this hand wrote in plaster and, when the hand disappeared, the writing was very real. And Belshazzar wasn't the only witness. A thousand people stopped in shock and saw the impossible. No wonder he turned pale with fright! Disembodied hands don't just appear and write on a wall. And yet, that's just what happened.

Now we catch up with Daniel, no longer a court favorite. It took a member of the older generation, Belshazzar's mother, to remember and recommend him. I suspect that the spectacular nature of this event is the only thing that could have induced this king to call for Daniel, who had been out of the public eye for a time. Obviously, his reputation was still intact. Don't you wonder what Daniel did during the years between chapters 4 and 5? We'll discover clues later on when we read about some of his visions during that in-between time. We know this for certain—He continued to follow His God.

Sharon's Verse(s): "Suddenly, they saw the fingers of a human hand writing on the plaster wall of the king's palace, near the lampstand. The king himself saw the hand as it wrote, and his face turned pale with fright. His knees knocked together in fear and his legs gave way beneath him" (Daniel 5:5-6). I chose two verses because they "fit" together. Have you done that a time or two? Sometimes you need more than one to fully express a thought.

Sharon's Response: I cannot even imagine how creepy it would be to see a hand . . . writing . . . on a wall! Oh, You got their attention, Lord. Real fear and real terror struck that entire gathering. How does a human king . . . no matter how proud and reckless . . . combat a hand . . . just a hand . . . that writes and then disappears? I guess no human messenger would have sufficed. Belshazzar would not have listened. He obviously had no regard for sacred things. But this? This had no rational explanation. This stopped the king and caused him to tremble. *Lord, how I praise You that You are able to capture anyone's attention! I pray that You would get the attention of _____. Help him to see You, Lord, and turn from the destructive path he's on. In Jesus' Name, Amen.*

What about you? Is someone in your life on the wrong path? Does your heart ache for him or her to return to the Light or find the Light for the first time? Stop and pray right now. God is able to reach any individual. Ask God to break through and create a softened heart, so that when He speaks, as with Belshazzar, he or she will start asking questions.

Daniel 5:18-31

We left Daniel in quite the predicament yesterday. He's standing in a banquet hall with a wine-filled king who has just been terrorized by an armless hand and words he can't understand. Daniel is promised an abundance of marvelous rewards: purple robes, gold chains, and high rank. Somehow, I don't think any of that moved Daniel at all. I'm guessing he does not want or need more purple robes or gold chains.

So here's this good man, having now lived in Babylon over 60 years, facing a corrupt and calloused king—knowing that king is about to die. And Daniel is the one who must deliver the news . . . that Babylon is about to be invaded. A lesser man might be tempted to say nothing, especially since the invasion is literally underway beneath the city as they speak. But Daniel is a truth teller, and he works for One. And *only* that One.

Dig in to the Scripture, friend, and marvel at Daniel's boldness as he explains the meaning of the strange words written on that wall. Imagine yourself in a place where God asks you to deliver a difficult message to one who will be less than pleased to hear it. Would you be quietly praying, asking for God's help? I'm pretty sure I'd be begging for God's help!

Dear Lord, please teach us as we read. Help us to "see" what You want us to see as we read this passage of Your Word. In Jesus' Name, Amen.

My Reflections

Request:

Seek the verse you wish to ponder.

Read: Daniel 5:18-31

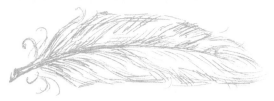

Write out your verse, still seeking the Lord to illuminate and teach.

Record:

Write what you learned from your reading. Does the verse help you with any current life situation? Is there a lesson here you can tuck away for a difficult time yet to come?

Respond:

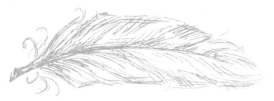

Sharon's Reflections

I love imagining Daniel, older now than the young man I've pictured so far in our readings, calmly explaining the writing on the wall to the frightened king. Daniel doesn't want gifts, and he knows for a fact that life is about to change irrevocably for Babylon. After the chaos of the imminent invasion, robes and chains will have little meaning. However, even at this late point in Belshazzar's life, it seems he has a chance to repent. Daniel reminds him of all that he knew about the living God of Israel from the stories of King Nebuchadnezzar. The past was not so far removed from him that he was unaware of the madness of his predecessor and his return to sanity.

These were King Belshazzar's last hours. Daniel made that very clear. I'm puzzled by the king's response. He gives Daniel gifts he doesn't want and puts him in charge again, third in command. Did he do this out of fear? Did he hope to appease the God who wrote on the wall? Did he figure it couldn't hurt to honor an old man? Only God knows Belshazzar's motives. We can trust that God dealt with Belshazzar in full justice and mercy, perfectly meting out what was due and what was right. I wonder what would have happened if Belshazzar had repented? (Actually, it's possible he did repent. Only God knows his thoughts in the last hours of his life.)

Somehow, in the invasion that night, Belshazzar was killed but Daniel was not. God wasn't finished with him yet, as we'll see in Chapter 6. Darius the Mede takes over Babylon at the age of 62. As I write this, I'm also 62, so I have to admit I find it all quite encouraging. Many wonderful things can be done at every age. I hope you too, whatever your age, will still be serving faithfully, like Daniel, throughout all the days of life God grants you.

Sharon's Verse: "You are his successor, O Belshazzar, and you knew all this, yet you have not humbled yourself." —Daniel 5:22

Sharon's Response: *I was wondering why King Nebuchadnezzar was given longer to repent and was allowed insanity and recovery rather than death while Belshazzar was told he would die that very night. This verse helps me understand, Lord. Belshazzar knew all that had happened to his predecessor. He knew about Nebuchadnezzar's pride and how he was humbled. He knew all this, and he even knew it was the God of Israel who had humbled Nebuchadnezzar. But instead of learning from his predecessor, he flagrantly went out of his way to defy the God of Israel. This did not work out well for Belshazzar. Father God, You will not be mocked. You can humble any man or woman You choose. You hold all our lives in Your wise, omnipotent hands. I bow my head in worship.*

Daniel 6:1-15

It's hard to imagine the shake-up that took place when King Darius the Mede conquered Babylon. According to the ancient historian, Herodotus, it was pretty much a bloodless battle. The Medes crept in under the city and simply took charge, quickly and completely. King Belshazzar was killed and that would certainly have made it easier for a new power to declare himself the ruler. It seems the people of Babylon simply realigned themselves and obeyed their new master.

Interestingly, Daniel, now in his eighties, is chosen to serve under Darius. Was this because the officials at that banquet recounted to the new rulers that Daniel had proclaimed their victory before anyone else even knew about it? Perhaps. Possibly King Darius wanted administrators from Nebuchadnezzar's time because they would know the history of the kingdom. Whatever the reason, Daniel is obviously still fully capable of administrative work even at eighty-something years.

Daniel has now lived through the reigns of Nebuchadnezzar and his successors and is serving a fourth ruler, King Darius. Watch for the key decision Daniel made in his daily routine that reveals why he was the faithful, righteous man that he was.

Dear Lord, we sit here with our Bibles open, so thankful for Your living Word. You are our Sovereign King, and we look to You for nourishment for our souls and wisdom to live well in service to You. Teach us, Lord, for Your servants are listening. In Jesus' Name, Amen.

My Reflections

Request:

Read the passage through twice, seeking "your" verse for the day.

Read: Daniel 6:1-15

Write out your verse.

Record:

Respond: Write a response to the Lord.

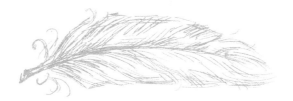

Sharon's Reflections

Once again we find Daniel excelling in everything he touches. In his new role as one of three men selected to supervise 120 provinces, his ability was so great that King Darius noticed. In fact, Daniel was so trusted by the king that plans were made to put him directly in charge of the entire empire. Wow. That's a ton of responsibility for a man who started out a teenaged captive in a foreign land. What a life Daniel lived! Certainly not the one he might have chosen, but rich in knowledge and adventure and the serious work of caring for the welfare of the most extensive empire of the time.

In this passage, we see the pivotal decision Daniel made in his daily routine, a choice God honored by giving him great success and competence. I believe that this one decision to stay close to God through a daily rhythm of prayer and worship is what led to his ability to stand uncorrupted throughout his lifetime. What's so inspiring is that we can do this too! Let's learn from Daniel and contemplate our own lives. What habits have you and I established in our day-to-day routine that keep worship and prayer and the

reading of the Word present each day? I think about the simple act of praying before a meal, acknowledging our God as the Provider and thanking Him for every bite we eat. I think of this study. We're meeting with God in a special way each day. We're studying His Word. We're praying and listening. These are the rhythms that God will use to build in us a dependence on Him that will steady us in the hardest of times. Let's hold fast to them so that we may hold fast to the God who loves us and who is with us, just as He was with Daniel, giving us strength and courage to do what is right.

I also find it interesting that someone can simply be minding his own business, doing his work well, and still be disliked and criticized. If you have ever been unjustly maligned or unfairly judged, you will identify with Daniel. Be encouraged, dear one. It truly is possible to be treated poorly simply because you are doing what is right. Jesus has this to say about those who are persecuted because of righteousness: "God blesses those who are persecuted for doing right, for the Kingdom of Heaven is theirs. God blesses you when people mock you and persecute you and lie about you and say all sorts of evil things against you because you are my followers. Be happy about it! Be very glad! For a great reward awaits you in heaven. And remember, the ancient prophets were persecuted in the same way" (Matthew 5:10-12).

Yes, remember ancient prophets like our Daniel and be glad. You are in the best of company.

Sharon's Verse: "Daniel soon proved himself more capable than all the other administrators and high officers. Because of Daniel's great ability, the king made plans to place him over the entire empire." —Daniel 6:3

Sharon's Response: *This teenaged Israelite captive, now nearing the end of his earthly life, is a key advisor of the Medo-Persian Empire. Wow. Father, the diet that he adhered to way back in the day when he refused to compromise on Your food laws must have kept him healthy and fit. His mind is still sharp, by Your grace, and it seems he still has the respectful "presence" that made him a friend of kings. He reminds me of Joseph—both were men of principle. Both were taken away from their native land of Israel. Both were always faithful to honor You and to work hard no matter what and no matter where. Father, I want to finish well like these two. Not necessarily in charge of anything (!) but always faithful . . . honoring You to my last breath . . . working hard in Your vineyards for Your Kingdom that is to come. Help me, please, to serve You well all my days. In Jesus' Name, Amen.*

Daniel 6:16-28

Yesterday, we watched a brave man, who was being attacked and undermined, continue to kneel boldly in plain sight of those who would take him down for that very act. How I love the picture that comes to mind of him kneeling—by an open window, for crying out loud—where everyone can see his worship of the one true God! Daniel kept being Daniel despite persecution and even with the full knowledge that the punishment would be a gruesome death. His loyalty to God never wavered. In fact, his enemies used his faithfulness to God as a trap because they couldn't ensnare him any other way.

We live in a time and place in our country right now in which we can worship without much fear. Ominous signs, though, indicate that a shift may be coming. With more frequent shootings in churches, for instance, will we still choose to go each Sunday, declaring that day the Lord's Day and meeting with fellow believers? Many of our brothers and sisters in other lands risk their lives when they meet together. And yet meet together they do, adhering to the command in Hebrews 10:25 not to forsake that practice. What if a time comes when Christianity is outlawed? Will we continue to openly serve our Lord Jesus? If it means going to prison, if it means torture like that den of lions, will we still follow Him then?

I know this for sure: I will need God's strength to carry me if such a time comes upon us in my lifetime. I have no strength on my own. I will ask Him for His. And I know this for sure: if we literally choose the lions' den for the sake of Christ, we will triumph in the end. I hold onto the powerful words of Scripture in Romans 8:18, "Yet what we suffer now is nothing compared to the glory he will reveal to us later." It will be worth it all. Someday we'll be with our Lord in Heaven, with Daniel and countless faithful ones, and "He will wipe every tear from [our] eyes. There will be no more death or mourning or crying or pain, for the old order of things has passed away" (Revelation 21:4 NIV).

Dear Lord, we choose You now, and we choose You always, through easy times and through hard times. Where else would we go? You made us. You will sustain us. In You we find our joy. Teach us from this passage of Scripture.

My Reflections

Request:

Read the passage twice, seeking "your" verse for the day.

Read: Daniel 6:16-28

Write out your verse.

Record:

Write a response to the Lord.

Respond:

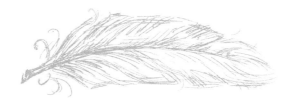

Sharon's Reflections

I find it interesting that King Darius was trapped by his own ruling. He allowed the administrators to appeal to his vanity and did not think through the consequences. He surely did not want Daniel to die. He must have felt like the biggest fool to have been tricked like that. Still, he adhered to the immutable law for it was an ironclad rule that once a formal law had been made, it must be followed and could not be changed. So we see King Darius pacing and fretting the night away, while our friend Daniel spent his night in awe among lions that did not harm him in any way.

I wonder what Daniel was thinking when he was thrown to the lions? Did he see the angel shut the lions' mouths? He must have been stunned! Did he feel God's hands gently

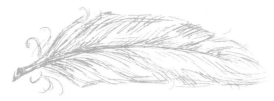

lower him to the floor so that he landed with not a bone broken or an ankle twisted? Did he quickly realize that all would be well? Did he feel a sense of calm and peace? Oh, what a night of worship he must have spent among the lions with his Savior and Lord! What a wondrous night, when his God was so clearly with him!

We can rest in this assurance, friend. If terrible times come, God will be with us. He will be there in the midst and give us all we need to stand firm. Whether we are rescued or not, He will never leave us or forsake us, and He will see us safely through. What an amazing God we serve!

Sharon's Verse: "My God sent his angel to shut the lions' mouths so that they would not hurt me, for I have been found innocent in his sight. And I have not wronged you, Your Majesty." —Daniel 6:22

Sharon's Response: *I love how Daniel gives You glory, God, and how he shows deep respect for the king. It's a great model for me to follow. You alone are worthy of worship and praise! You alone do miracles. And on an earthly level, it pleases You when we respect the authorities over us. Help me to live like Daniel.*

Did you notice the ending to this unbelievable story? First of all, the mockers met their Maker, didn't they? Those lions were genuinely hungry, and without the aid of an angel, the troublemakers and their families suffered and died in that lions' den. Yes, their families died too. Isn't that the sad reality of evil? The consequences don't just affect the evildoers, but those close to them often suffer as well. Second, Darius became a believer in Daniel's God and put out a new proclamation. Like Nebuchadnezzar before him, he acknowledged God's supremacy and right to rule. Darius was humbled through Daniel's witness and God's protection that night. His language was clear, "I decree that everyone throughout my kingdom should tremble with fear before the God of Daniel. For he is the living God, and he will endure forever. His kingdom will never be destroyed, and his rule will never end" (Daniel 6:26).

Here we are millennia later. The kingdom of the Medes and Persians is long gone. Other kingdoms have risen and fallen just as Daniel predicted when he interpreted the dream of the large statue. And hundreds of other kingdoms. But our God and His Kingdom remain. And we worship Him to this day. Our God reigns. What a wonderful truth!

Daniel 7:1-14

Today, we turn a corner and enter the strange world of visions and dreams, of angels and spiritual beings, of prophecy and prayers. So far, we've studied Daniel chronologically in history. We've seen him consistently maintain integrity and wisdom and right choices over and over again. It's been quite wonderful and inspiring. I've gathered strength in my own life from studying his life, strength to live uprightly in our own increasingly pagan culture.

The next section of the book of Daniel unfolds a series of dreams and visions that God allowed Daniel to see at various times in his life. The one we're looking at today transpired around 555 B.C. Since Daniel was captured as a teen in 605 B.C., he would have been about 65 years old at the time of this strange dream. Personally, I'm more comfortable reading history and stories about people's lives than I am with mysterious dreams and visions. However, I absolutely believe God's Word is true—and that means all of it.

We read in 2 Timothy 3:16-17 that "*All* Scripture is inspired by God and is useful to teach us what is true and to make us realize what is wrong in our lives. It corrects us when we are wrong and teaches us to do what is right. God uses it to prepare and equip his people to do every good work" (emphasis mine). That word "all" means that every single book in the Bible and every single verse hold significance for us. As we dig into this harder passage, let's trust God and ask Him to teach us from His Word. I believe He will.

Dear Lord, as for me, I'm not an expert in visions. I don't hold a degree in biblical studies, but for each of us, as we come to You simply as Christians who trust You to reveal Your truth to us, we ask that You will use Your words in our lives to help us live correctly. Teach us, Lord, as we come to You eager to learn from Your Word in Daniel. In Jesus' Name, Amen.

My Reflections

Request:

Read through twice, seeking "your" verse for the day.

Read: Daniel 7:1-14

Write out your verse.

Record:

Write a response to the Lord.

Respond:

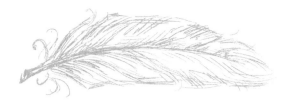

Sharon's Reflections

I can't imagine what it must have been like to dream this dream. Some quality about it must have differentiated it from a typical dream or nightmare—more intense, more real, more startling. Daniel recognized that the dream originated from God, so he called it a vision and recorded it for others to read—including you and me.

Not a pretty sight, is it? Great lion-like creatures and bears with ribs hanging from their mouths. Multi-headed beasts that frighten and devour. I can say with absolute certainty that I would not want to dream this dream or see this vision! (Although . . . I suppose . . . if God sent such a vision to me, I would receive it. He does know best.)

God chose to reveal to Daniel these visions of things yet to come. It's important for us to remember that God is not bound by time. God isn't worrying and wondering what the future holds. He's beyond the confines of time and sees the beginning and the end all at once. He reveals the future to Daniel in this dream as He would unroll a scroll already written. For a finite, little woman like me, it's super hard to wrap my mind around the

concept of timelessness and God's ability to be outside of time. I'm wired for time as a human being on this planet. As David says in Psalm 139:6, "Such knowledge is too wonderful for me, too great for me to understand!"

But when you ponder the fact that God is beyond our understanding, it's actually immensely comforting. If a finite mind like mine could explain Him, then He would surely not be the Most High Being that He absolutely is. I celebrate His greatness. I'm grateful He knows the future as a sure and certain fact on which I can count. This is actually very good news. Aren't you glad He knows the end of the story and can assure us that it is good . . . no matter how hard the middle might get? I am. I'm even glad He doesn't sugarcoat the hard parts. If He did, how shocked we would be when dictators arise and wreak havoc on the world! But He has prepared us for trouble and turmoil. Throughout Scripture, He makes these things very clear: In this world we will have trouble; He has overcome the trouble; and He gives us peace. Hear Jesus' words in John 16:33, "I have told you these things, so that in me you may have peace. In this world you will have trouble. But take heart! I have overcome the world." We have no need for fear. Jesus has overcome!

Sharon's Verse: "I watched as thrones were put in place and the Ancient One sat down to judge. His clothing was as white as snow, his hair like purest wool. He sat on a fiery throne with wheels of blazing fire." —Daniel 7:9

Sharon's Response: *After reading the dreams about horrifying and all-consuming beasts, this verse comes as a refreshing assurance. The Ancient One will sit down to judge. A day of judgment is coming. Although kingdoms and rulers will have come into power and fallen from power, You, O Lord God, will remain. The great I Am . . . always . . . always . . . is. Oh, God of Heaven, how I praise You! You will judge rightly on that day, with mercy toward all who love You and ask for Your rescue. Amen.*

How good it is to belong to the King of kings! I love that He does not change. When we give our lives into His care, He becomes our Shepherd . . . forever. No matter what happens . . . illness, disappointment, hardship, war . . . no matter what happens, we are His and will be kept in His care. He declares in John 10:27-28, "My sheep listen to my voice; I know them, and they follow me. I give them eternal life, and they will never perish. No one can snatch them away from me." Hallelujah and Amen!

Daniel 7:15-28

Did you notice the glimpse of Jesus we were allowed in our last reading? He shows up as the "son of man." In fact, Jesus loves this particular name for Himself and uses it often when He speaks to people in the New Testament. Here are Daniel's words from his God-given dream:

> As my vision continued that night, I saw someone like a son of man coming with the clouds of heaven. He approached the Ancient One and was led into his presence. He was given authority, honor, and sovereignty over all the nations of the world, so that people of every race and nation and language would obey him. His rule is eternal—it will never end. His kingdom will never be destroyed. —Daniel 7:13-14

Yes! Jesus shows up in Daniel's vision. Messiah! Savior! Ruler! King! Right after all the terror of the beasts and the fearfulness of the great throne with the Ancient One, here comes Jesus, our Savior. Daniel was not left in terror. He was shown the Victor. Only Satan leaves us in fear and terror. God brings peace and victory and reassurance. And it's worth noting that when Jesus used the title for Himself, "son of man," the teachers of the law and the Pharisees in Jesus' day knew exactly what He meant. He was declaring himself to be the one Daniel described . . . Messiah, Savior, Ruler, and King!

In today's verses we gain insight into the meaning of this vision. Daniel certainly needs an explanation—and he boldly asks for it. This is one more character trait that I love about our man Daniel. When he doesn't understand something . . . he asks. God tells us to "Ask and it will be given to you; seek and you will find; knock and the door will be opened to you" (Matthew 7:7 NIV). It's okay to ask. It's okay to tell God when you don't understand. Learn from Daniel. When you're confused and bothered, don't walk away from God. He's the only sure source of wisdom. Walk toward Him, seeking help in understanding. And if you don't understand right away? Trust that you will in God's good time, because you have asked. Let's pray and then turn to our passage and see Daniel requesting and receiving the vision's interpretation.

Dear Lord, please forgive us when we walk away from You due to a lack of understanding. Help us to always come toward You . . . ever closer . . . asking You for help and trusting and waiting for the answers. We come asking for Your wisdom and a word from You that will help us live our day well. Please show us through this passage. In Your Name, Amen.

149

My Reflections

Request:

Find a verse that strikes you. It can be one that is clear in meaning. It could be one that puzzles you. Write it down in any case and talk to the Lord about it. Remember, you can always seek more information from good Bible commentaries or from your pastor or other leaders in your church. Seek and you will find!

Read: Daniel 7:15-28

Write out your verse.

Record:

Write a response to the Lord.

Respond:

Sharon's Reflections

In his vision, Daniel was able to talk and ask questions. And because he didn't understand, he asks someone standing near the throne. Was that someone an angel? The Bible doesn't say, but it seems likely. In Daniel 7:10, we read that millions of angels were there. Oh, what a sight that must have been! What would it be like as a human being to find yourself in an unearthly place, surrounded by creatures too wonderful to comprehend for whom you had no conceivable reference?! Wow.

I love that the angel assures Daniel twice that "in the end" the kingdom of the Most High God will be an everlasting Kingdom. He states it right at the beginning of his explanation and again at the end. In between, he lets Daniel know that hard things will come.

We know that many already have come to pass. Great rulers and nations have, indeed, risen and fallen. Millions of innocent people have been crushed over the centuries, and we still see oppression in our world today. Consider all the refugees, lost without a homeland because of war and destruction.

The Bible is true. It doesn't paint rosy, unrealistic pictures of life. It doesn't shy away from the sad truth that evil exists in a world where sin is alive and active in human lives. Yet living in today's world, even in the midst of the madness, we see pockets of peace. I can choose to be worried about the economy. I can fret over viruses and mysterious diseases and the cancer that strikes so many without warning. I can work myself into a tizzy over bad politicians and scary dictators who might send a nuclear bomb my way. But that would be foolish. How much better to find peace in the moment, noticing the beauty God's world still has to offer. Admiring stars in a quiet sky, feeling the warmth of sun on my cheeks, worshiping the One who is still present in the chaos are much better choices, aren't they? We need to be aware of the troubles, yes, but we don't have to dwell on them. Paul instructs us to fix our minds on "whatever is true, whatever is noble, whatever is right, whatever is pure, whatever is lovely, whatever is admirable—if anything is excellent or praiseworthy—think about such things" (Philippians 4:8 NIV).

Sharon's Verse: "But in the end, the holy people of the Most High will be given the kingdom and they will rule forever and ever." —Daniel 7:18

Sharon's Response: *Thank You, Lord, for Your reassurance in verses 18 and 27 that in the end You will be victorious, Your Kingdom will be established for eternity. The beasts in Daniel's vision are terrifying, arrogant, and destructive, yet they do not last. You, the Most High God will reign forever, and those of us who are Your "holy people"—holy only because Jesus paid the price for us—will inherit the Kingdom. I love that You are Most High. No one, no "god," compares to You. You reign supreme. I love that I am called "holy"—set apart because of Your grace. Washed clean and with a glorious future ahead of me. Thank You.*

Be thankful, dear one. God has prepared us for the trials and tribulations that come in this world. When we face hard times, we don't need to be surprised or fret about whether He's in charge. Be full of gladness that He will be with us always, no matter what. And then live your life well. Enjoy the "pockets of peace" and the beauty of the world around you. "Feel" the arms of the Shepherd who loves you surrounding you, holding you. Rest in knowing it ends very, very well indeed.

Daniel 8:1-14

We now turn to another vision Daniel chooses to share with us. This vision came to him two years after the last one. Honestly, I had the mistaken idea that Daniel was forever having visions, but no, not true. They actually came rarely, but with such force and clarity, that he recognized them as being sent directly from God.

Once again the vision concerns a dire prophecy about a future time when even the temple will not be safe. It's interesting to note that at the time Daniel had this vision, the first temple built by Solomon had already been destroyed. As we look into the future with Daniel in this passage, imagine what this part of the vision would have meant to him: the temple would be rebuilt at some point!

As a matter of fact, since Daniel's day the temple has been rebuilt twice. In about 538 B.C., King Cyrus issued a decree that the temple was to be rebuilt as described in the book of Ezra. Again, shortly before Jesus' time on earth, King Herod completely refurbished and expanded the temple into the magnificent structure in which Jesus walked and taught. That temple was destroyed in 70 A.D.

This cyclical building and destruction of the temple is a parable of the way we humans often live. We draw close to God and then we walk away. And then we draw close again. Thankfully, now that we have the Holy Spirit residing within us, our very bodies are God's temple. What an amazing thought! God indwells us. Paul admonishes us to treat our bodies as the sacred vessels they are. In 1 Corinthians 6:19-20 we read, "Don't you realize that your body is the temple of the Holy Spirit, who lives in you and was given to you by God? You do not belong to yourself, for God bought you with a high price. So you must honor God with your body."

Dear Lord, thank You for the astounding presence of the Holy Spirit in our lives. How amazing to think that when we receive You as Lord and Savior, You enter our very being, helping us from the inside to know You and serve You and honor You. Please illuminate Your Word to us as we read. Teach us, Lord. In Jesus' Name we pray, Amen.

My Reflections

Request:

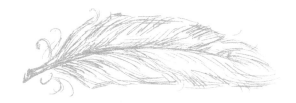

Find your verse. This is such an interesting passage. I wish we were sitting together. I'd love to know which one you choose from this section and why!

Read: Daniel 8:1-14

Write out your verse.

Record:

Write a response to the Lord.

Respond:

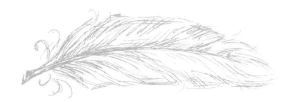

Sharon's Reflections

Wow. Reading this vision creates a very chaotic and frightening picture in my mind. First, we see a ram with two long horns. This ram does just as he pleases and no one could stop him. That's scary. But then he is stopped—and suddenly I can breathe again. You see, even earthly rulers who seem unstoppable . . . are not. They don't last.

Next comes the goat, and he's now running the show. However, a part of the goat breaks off and takes over being in charge. And once again, I see the pattern that has been consistent throughout the book of Daniel. Nations rise and fall. Rulers come and go. They are frightening, yes. They do not last. Ever. Hallelujah, our God is greater!

Daniel sees real, unrestrained power from the enemy for a time, as he watches the future unfold in this vision. The Temple is defiled, and truth itself is overthrown. What a horrible thought! No one valued truth. Oh, dear God, that sounds sadly like the trend in our culture today.

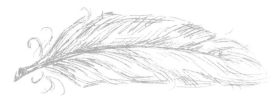

Next comes the age-old question, asked in times of trouble, "How long?" The question is posed by a "holy one," I'm assuming an angel, and the reply is a "number of days." Then, in the last verse of our reading, we come to that beautiful and encouraging phrase, "the Temple will be made right again" (vs. 14).

We are reassured once more that no matter how dreadful the world around us becomes, even if truth itself seems to disappear, all will be made right again. Nothing can stand against our God. In fact, the only reason the calamities in this vision are allowed is because God, for His own sovereign purposes, restrains Heaven's army. Oh, friend, do I understand all this? Not at all. Do I understand enough to take courage? Yes! God wins. Struggles will occur, hardship will come, but God wins. That's good enough for me.

Sharon's Verse: "The army of heaven was restrained from responding to this rebellion. So the daily sacrifice was halted, and truth was overthrown. The horn succeeded in everything it did" —Daniel 8:12

Sharon's Response: *Father God, what a relief to read this! If the army of Heaven had not been restrained, that evil "horn" would not have prospered. I don't understand why You allow evil men times of power and terrorizing. But I'm comforted to know that it's only because You choose to restrain Heaven's army. I'm reassured that You are still in charge, still able to bring down anyone or anything at any time. You delay Your return for Your good reasons. But You will return. And win! I rest in that.*

Here's an interesting fact about the book of Daniel. It's written in two different languages. Chapter 1 through 2:4 is written in Hebrew. Then, Daniel 2:5 through the end of chapter 7 is written in Aramaic. Now we are in chapter 8, where the writing reverts back to Hebrew and continues until the end of the book in chapter 12. I checked with the International Bible Society to try and understand why, and this is what I found:

> Theories vary, but a lot of folks think that the portions of the book of Daniel intended specifically for Jews were written in Hebrew, while portions with a broader message to the nations were written in the language used across that world for diplomacy and commerce, which was Aramaic. (www.biblica.com/articles/7-fascinating-facts-that-will-change-how-you-read-the-book-of-daniel)

So there's that. In case you were curious.

Daniel 8:15-27

Instead of leaving Daniel in the middle of chapter 8, we'll postpone our scheduled two-day break until tomorrow. If you're like me, you don't want a break right in the middle of this chapter, right in the middle of Daniel's vision. It's too suspenseful . . . we need to hear what it means!

I find it interesting that these visions, seen in Daniel's fifties during the reign of King Belshazzar, were written in Hebrew. It seems probable that they were meant for God's people and not for the Babylonians at large. Perhaps the tales of nations rising and falling would not have gone over well with Belshazzar. As you recall, right up until the night he died, Belshazzar was confident that he would rule forever—feasting and drinking and desecrating temple items while the Medes snuck in to his city and killed him. I suspect Belshazzar would not have been all that excited about Daniel's visions. But living in Babylon were many other Israelites. Like Daniel, they too had been captured and brought against their will from their homeland. They too longed for Jerusalem. They too likely prayed facing Jerusalem, and Daniel's visions, including a restored temple, would have been a great comfort to them. Their God was no longer silent, but speaking again through Daniel.

I love that God continues to speak to us—through His Word. Our access to the Bible is one of our most precious blessings. At any time we can sit down and open up the Bible and hear the living God speak through its pages. That's phenomenal. That's breathtaking. That's why we're doing this Bible study. How I hope you decide with me that the most important thing we can do is spend set-apart time with the One who loves us! The unchanging, unalterable priority of our lives should be our times with God in His Word and prayer. Period. So . . . let's dig in and see what's next with our stunned friend Daniel as he tries to absorb the vision and comprehend the bizarre events that were shown him.

Dear Lord, as we open our Bibles—this amazing book—we sit in awe that we hold Your very words in our hands. Oh, Father, forgive us for the times we neglect to meet with You. Thank You for grace in this. Help us to hear Your voice as we study. Teach us, Lord, please. In Jesus' Name, Amen.

My Reflections

Request:

Read through twice and find your special verse for the day.

Read: Daniel 8:15-27

Write out your verse.

Record:

Write a response to the Lord.

Respond:

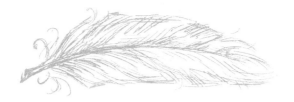

Sharon's Reflections

As I pondered this passage, I have to admit to some relief when I read the last part of the last verse in Chapter 8. ". . . I [Daniel] was greatly troubled by the vision and could not understand it" (vs. 27b). Even after an angel had explained the meaning, much was still too hard for Daniel to comprehend. That definitely comforts my own feelings of inadequacy as I read these visions and explanations. I glean what I can, and then I tell myself that if I'm still alive during the very end times, perhaps I will learn even more should I see the events unfolding.

Let's talk about angels. Did you realize that very few angels are actually introduced by name in Scripture? The angel who comes to Daniel is Gabriel. Wow. Gabriel is the angel chosen by God to be a messenger to Mary the mother of Jesus. He had the high privilege of coming to this young teen girl to reveal the incredible promise that she would be the one to carry the Messiah in her womb. Gabriel had also been sent to Zechariah with news that he would be father to John the Baptist, the great forerunner of the Christ.

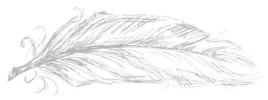

Another fact we learn about angels in Scripture is that they are terrifying. In Luke 1:12 we read, "Zechariah was shaken and overwhelmed with fear when he saw him." Daniel writes about his encounter with Gabriel, ". . . I became so terrified that I fell with my face to the ground . . ." (Daniel 8:17b). When Gabriel spoke, Daniel actually fainted and had to be revived. Teenage Mary fared better than both of these older men. The Bible tells us in Luke 1:29 that Mary was "confused and disturbed." Their reactions let us know that the sight of Gabriel was terrifying—definitely not of our world or like anything these three had ever seen.

A third truth we learn about angels from our glimpses of Gabriel is that he is good. He reassured Mary and Zechariah. When Daniel fainted dead away, Gabriel reached out with a touch and lifted Daniel to his feet. One day, we too will see Gabriel in Heaven. That will be something . . . but will pale in significance to the great sight of our Lord and King Jesus seated on the throne! Oh, what a day that will be!

Gabriel was and still is a messenger for God, and in all three visits mentioned above, he came to speak the exact words God had given him. Gabriel explains the vision to Daniel—and his words are filled with reassurance. Daniel is repeatedly told that the events of his vision will not take place during his lifetime. I have to admit, I'm not eager for these events to happen in my lifetime, but I'm content to leave those decisions in God's wise hands. He chooses the times in which we live just as He chose for Daniel to live out a life of faith far from his homeland. Who am I to tell God what He should choose for me? I can simply hold His big hand tightly and trust Him. You can too.

Sharon's Verse: "Then I, Daniel, was overcome and lay sick for several days. Afterward I got up and performed my duties for the king, but I was greatly troubled by the vision and could not understand it." —Daniel 8:27

Sharon's Response: *Oh, Father God, that vision shook Daniel to the core. And meeting with an angel did too. Evidently in our human bodies we mortals can't handle too much sight of the spiritual realm. It makes sense to me that Daniel suffered from the shock of it for several days. Yet You chose to reveal these end-time scenes to him, Lord. And as I read them, I grasp that kingdoms will rise and fall and that worse is coming before the end . . . but I do not fully understand either. Lord, these things seem "too big" for me. Thank You that they are not too big for You. Please teach me what I need to know. And help me trust You with all the rest.*

I do hope that God has been speaking to you through these visions and dreams of Daniel's. I hope you know how dearly He loves you. You are safe with Him and nowhere else. Rest in that today.

Psalm 2

I had no idea how profoundly relevant Psalm 2 would be to our recent look at the rise and fall of kingdoms in Daniel. Yet the topic of today's psalm concerns the nations, their disrespect for God, and the multitudes that believe they can live without God—all to their ultimate chagrin. I love the way God weaves for us the right theme at the right time.

In your life I'm sure, as in mine, are individuals who don't believe in God. How my heart aches for them! Some are deeply wounded from a tragedy God has allowed in their lives. They blame Him—even while declaring they don't believe He exists! And yet think about it. If we lose a loved one and then grow so angry we refuse to believe in God, we also lose all hope of seeing our loved one ever again. We lose the comfort of the Comforter Himself, who enters into our pain and weeps with us. (See John 11:33-35.)

If you long for loved ones to know God, pray for them. Pray for them for days, years, and decades if need be. Pray for them to find God before they die and meet Him. For meet Him they will. A day will come when "every knee [will] bow, in heaven and on earth and under the earth, and every tongue declare that Jesus Christ is Lord, to the glory of God the Father" (Philippians 2:10b-11).

I've seen God touch individuals at the very end of their days. I witnessed one, breathing slowly and irregularly, suddenly wake up and tell me she saw Christ. There is always hope, dear one, that He will reach them at the very last. So pray.

But you must not forget this one thing, dear friends: A day is like a thousand years to the Lord, and a thousand years is like a day. The Lord isn't really being slow about his promise, as some people think. No, he is being patient for your sake. He does not want anyone to be destroyed, but wants everyone to repent. —2 Peter 3:8-9

Dear Lord, please show us a word from You as we read.

My Reflections

Request:

Read through twice and find your special verse of the day.

Read: Psalm 2

Write out your verse.

Record:

Write a response to the Lord.

Respond:

Sharon's Reflections

I love the question the psalmist asks at the very beginning of Psalm 2, "Why are the nations so angry? Why do they waste their time with futile plans?" (vs. 1). Oh, how fruitless it seems when frantic, frenetic people endeavor to make their own plans work out just the way they want. Ultimately, what can we really control? We can't control the weather, natural disasters, economic failures, accidents, sickness, or death. Nope. The sooner we realize who does have that power and ask Him to be our Guide, the better off we will be.

This psalm invites us to ponder the fruitlessness of a life lived without God on a national scale as well as in our individual lives. We are given a peek into Heaven and God's response to the rebellion of the nations. Charles Swindoll writes this in his study Bible notes: "God finds it hilarious that any person or nation would raise their puny fist and challenge Him. 'All the people of the earth are nothing compared to him' (Dan. 4:35). What nation can stand against the Almighty who made them? The Lord laughs at the thought."

The kings of the earth and the rulers in this psalm accuse God of chaining them and enslaving them. Nothing could be further from the truth. God frees us. He breaks the bondage we are under to sin and disastrous decisions. He gently leads His flock. He helps us meet our fullest potential by giving us gifts of the Spirit to use with joy. Over and over, as we discovered in the Nest section of this book, God tells us and shows us that His love for us is deep, satisfying, and unchanging. The idea that God enslaves us is straight from Satan himself, who is the father of lies. He lied to Eve in the garden about God's plans and purposes, and he lies to this day. Let's not pay any attention to such foolishness. We know our God is good. We have seen His mercy and His compassion poured out on us. We are stunned that He loves us, even though He knows our most wicked moments. Only God satisfies. Let's drink from His living water and from no other stream.

Sharon's Verse: "But the one who rules in heaven laughs. The Lord scoffs at them." —Psalm 2:4

Sharon's Response: *Oh, good Shepherd of my soul, You are so much bigger than the nations who rage and the kings of the earth who plan and plot. They are like a tiny toddler whacking at his father's knees with a plastic sword. Seriously? No threat at all. I love that You are big. I love that You are mine, and I am Yours. Oh, the joy of it! Thank You, Lord.*

Several winters ago, a huge snowplow came roaring down our street, making one more sweep at the snow to widen our usable roadway. I had let my tiny, 14-pound dog, Bella, off leash, because I thought the plowing was done. But no! Off went that little dog lickety-split, barking and yipping at that plow. As she raced beside it, mere inches from the wheels that towered over her, my heart was in my throat. I ran after her shouting at the top of my lungs for her to stop. The plowman heard nothing. He just kept roaring down the road and around the corner he went with tiny Bella in fierce pursuit. Eventually, she came trotting back, confident that she had vanquished the "plow-beast." Eventually, my heart resumed its normal rate of beating. I think of that incident as I ponder this psalm. Could Bella, in a million years, have hurt that plow? No. Could that plow easily have crushed my foolish little puppy? Oh, yes. We are just as foolish as Bella when we yip at the heels of God—especially when we remember that He wants to pick us up in His big arms and love us and guide us. Let's acknowledge our littleness and happily nestle into His big and loving Goodness.

Proverbs 2

Our passage today encourages us to seek wisdom like treasure and cling to it. I commend you because you are seeking wisdom. Not because you're reading this book, but because through this book you're reading The Book—God's Word. I hope the words written in Proverbs 2 will grip you and spur you on to further growth in Christ. You will see urgency in this passage that comes from the heart of a parent talking to a child and desperately wanting that child to "get it right."

Before we read from Proverbs, I wish to share with you a New Testament passage on wisdom that has always astounded me. When I encountered this picture of wisdom in James many years ago, I was struck by what was not said. James' description of wisdom doesn't include memorizing wise books or attending seminary or following great teachers to glean from their words. This advice might be good for some of us, but certainly not for all of us. Instead, James describes wisdom like this:

> But the wisdom from above is first of all pure. It is also peace loving, gentle at all times, and willing to yield to others. It is full of mercy and the fruit of good deeds. It shows no favoritism and is always sincere. And those who are peacemakers will plant seeds of peace and reap a harvest of righteousness. —James 3:17-18

Looking at this passage confirms a truth about our God. He is always more interested in our character than in our service. The greatest things are the "being" things—who we really are in our inmost parts. If we desire wisdom, we must be pure, seekers of peace, gentle, and willing to yield, not clinging to our selfish desires. A wise person is full of mercy and from that come the good deeds. Those who are wise don't show favoritism, they are sincere, and they will reap a harvest of righteousness. Remember the story Jesus told about the ones who said to Him, "Lord, look at all we did for You!" And Jesus replies, "I never knew you." (See Matthew 7:21-23.) Yeah. First, we have to know Him. First, we must be filled on the inside with His Spirit and the fruit of His Spirit. That's wisdom. And from that wisdom will spring the good deeds, and they will bear good fruit.

Dear Lord, we desire to be wise, not foolish. Help us to read with intent and focus. Show us and teach us what You would have us learn. In Jesus' Name, Amen.

My Reflections

Request:

Read through twice and find your special verse of the day.

Read: Proverbs 2

Write out your verse.

Record:

Write a response to the Lord.

Respond:

Sharon's Reflections

Solomon's urgent desire that his children—or perhaps a particular son—should value wisdom and not behave foolishly shines through this chapter. And Solomon wants us to know that true wisdom springs from the knowledge of God. Knowing Him is at the heart of it all. With so many gems to choose from in this chapter, I wanted to underline most of the verses and had a hard time picking out just "one" verse!

In the second part of this chapter, Solomon gives an example of what happens when we won't listen to wisdom or seek to find it. The example is one that resonates today in this over-sexualized world of ours where pornography is easily found and watched by millions. Solomon knows that we will fall to temptation if we don't have a plan. If we are not rooted in wisdom and truth, the lure of the sensual will tug at us and lie to us.

Other lures, like the temptation to materialism, also seek to derail us. Our whole life can be shaped around buying that next and bigger house, making sure we have the latest fashions hanging in our closets, seeking out the best vacation spots, and buying the most expensive foods. Another example is the temptation to over medicate our pain through alcohol or prescription drugs or other drugs that lure and promise relief but instead create an insatiable, never-satisfied hunger for more and more until we are ruined.

The book of Proverbs is the cry of a loving parent begging his child to walk wisely and avoid the many traps of the enemy. We would do well to listen carefully and heed the warnings. Peter urges us in 1 Peter 5:8, "Stay alert! Watch out for your great enemy, the devil. He prowls around like a roaring lion, looking for someone to devour."

Sharon's Verse: "Wisdom will save you from evil people, from those whose words are twisted." —Proverbs 2:12

Sharon's Response: *Father God, protect me from twisted words! Help me to be discerning, to distinguish truth from lies and half-truths and innuendos. I don't want to be led astray. I want to "cry out for insight, and ask for understanding" (vs. 3) that I might live rightly with You. In Jesus name, I pray, Amen.*

Perhaps as you read this passage, you were struck by ways you have been deceived or led astray by the enemy of your soul. If that's the case, please listen carefully. You do not have to stay in that deceived place. God is able to rescue you from any addiction and any bondage. In fact, that's why Jesus came. To set you free! Confess honestly to God, and step off that wrong path and back onto the right one. Seek help from a wise friend or counselor. Yes, it may seem too scary to turn around . . . until you do. Once you confess your sin and ask for help, the immense relief that follows makes you wonder why on earth it ever took you so long. You are dearly loved by God. He loved you while you were a sinner, and Christ gave His life . . . died . . . for that sin. Walk away from it and grasp hold of the good hand of God. He'll lead you on that right path and give you wisdom that comes from knowing Him, wisdom that grows as you get to know Him better and better. I'm praying for each reader who seeks God through this book, and that includes . . . *you.*

Daniel 9:1-19

Today, we return to Daniel, this amazing book of history and prophecy. You'll notice in the first verse of chapter 9 that Daniel gives us the date when this part of his book was written. "It was the first year of the reign of Darius the Mede, the son of Ahasuerus, who became king of the Babylonians." This equates to 539 B.C. So in chapters 7 and 8, Daniel had walked us back in time to describe chronologically the visions and dreams God had previously revealed to him. Now he's ready to share with us the last great visions God enabled him to see.

Before we read those last visions, though, Daniel shares with us a surprising discovery he made while reading the scroll of Jeremiah, a prophet who was a contemporary of Daniel's. Jeremiah had prophesied the demise of Israel and its captivity. Since Daniel's discovery was in the first year of Darius' reign, I think we can presume it took place before Daniel was thrown in the lions' den. If we remember back to that event in Daniel 6, we see a close relationship between Darius and Daniel. "Hearing this, the king was deeply troubled, and he tried to think of a way to save Daniel. He spent the rest of the day looking for a way to get Daniel out of this predicament" (Daniel 6:14). I can't imagine that Darius would have reacted this way during the first year of his reign. He would not have known Daniel well enough at that point to be disturbed by his death. So . . . this discovery we are about to read would have preceded Daniel's lions' den test.

As a side note, I love that the Israelites brought with them sacred writings. They highly valued the Scriptures. This is one reason, among many, that we have the Bible in its preserved and highly accurate form today. God's Word was treasured from long ago by the remnant of His people who remained faithful. Daniel was certainly one of those, and as he read Jeremiah, he was stunned by what he read.

Heavenly Father, as we read about Daniel's discovery and the way Your Word came alive for him, may Your Word come alive for us. Teach us as we read. Help us to encounter fresh truth as Daniel did all those years ago. We yield ourselves to You and ask that Your Holy Spirit will guide us. In Jesus' mighty Name, Amen.

My Reflections

Request:

Read: Daniel 9:1-19

I think you will easily find a verse with so many great ones to choose from. (Wish we lived nearby, and you could tell me what you chose!)

Record:

Write a response to the Lord.

Respond:

Sharon's Reflections

Since Daniel was probably a teenager when Jerusalem was overthrown, and he's now around 80 years old . . . then the 70 years that Jeremiah predicted would elapse before Jerusalem was inhabited again . . . were just about over. WOW and wow! That was quite a discovery! Daniel must have been shaken and trembling as he wondered—is it possible that God will let His people return? Surely, that was impossible. King Darius certainly wasn't talking about letting everyone just wander on back to Israel!

If Daniel read Jeremiah from the beginning, he would eventually have come to this passage found in chapter 25 of our Bibles:

"This entire land will become a desolate wasteland. Israel and her neighboring lands will serve the king of Babylon for seventy years. Then, after the seventy years of captivity are over, I will punish the king of Babylon and his people for their sins," says the LORD. "I will make the country of the Babylonians a wasteland forever." —Jeremiah 25:11-12

Imagine Daniel's hope and joy as he began to do the math! Then he would have reached this passage, and his heart would have begun to thump in earnest:

This is what the LORD says: "You will be in Babylon for seventy years. But then I will come and do for you all the good things I have promised, and I will bring you home again. For I know the plans I have for you," says the LORD. "They are plans for good and not for disaster, to give you a future and a hope." —Jeremiah 29:10-11

No wonder Daniel fasted in sackcloth and ashes and cried out to God after he read these words. First, he repented for his people . . . then he pleaded with God for mercy and deliverance—the mercy and deliverance God seemed to be promising through the prophet Jeremiah.

By the way, just as Jeremiah had predicted, eventually Babylon was indeed punished, and that mighty city was swept away and buried for centuries under the desert sand.

Sharon's Verse: "O my God, lean down and listen to me. Open your eyes and see our despair. See how your city—the city that bears your name—lies in ruins. We make this plea, not because we deserve help, but because of your mercy." —Daniel 9:18

Sharon's Response: *Oh, the pleading in this prayer, dear Lord! And it was prayed in dead earnest in sackcloth and ashes by a fasting man. Daniel admits the unworthiness of God's people, but He knows You are merciful, Lord. So in trust, he appeals to You. Thank You for being a merciful God—the One I can also run to and ask for mercy.*

We read in the book of Ezra that God fulfilled the prophecy He had given through Jeremiah by stirring the heart of King Cyrus to make a proclamation that the Jewish people could return to Israel. What a miracle! And I find it most interesting that this proclamation was in the same timeframe as Daniel's miracle escape from the lions. Coincidence? I believe the two miracles could be related.

Yes, King Darius the Mede was responsible for the den of lions, and King Cyrus of Persia issued the proclamation, but we believe that King Cyrus took over very shortly after the great rescue from the lions. It's even thought by some that Darius and Cyrus had co-regency for a time. (See Daniel 6:28.) In any case, witnessing a Jewish captive rescued by his God had to make an impression on the king and could have been a factor in releasing all Daniel's kinsmen to return to their homeland.

What we do know for sure is that God knew for sure! In fact, if Daniel had also read the prophet Isaiah, he would have seen that Isaiah wrote about King Cyrus by name before he was even born! "When I say of Cyrus, 'He is my shepherd,' he will certainly do as I say. He will command, 'Rebuild Jerusalem'; he will say, 'Restore the Temple'" (Isaiah 44:28 and many other verses in Isaiah 44, 45, and 48).

Whether Daniel was aware of this or not, in the year 538 B.C., God stirred the heart of King Cyrus, and the return began—just as Isaiah and Jeremiah had predicted. I may not be able to figure out all the dates and sequences, but I see God's fingerprints all over this. God moved the heart of a king to bring about His own purposes and plans. And God honored the prayers of a faithful captive, our Daniel, whose life was a testimony to persistent, persevering prayer.

To learn more about this proclamation, read Ezra, chapter 1. In the rest of the book of Ezra and the book of Nehemiah, we learn that Zerubbabel, grandson of the last king of Judah, and the priest Jeshua were among the returning exiles who accomplished the rebuilding of the Temple. Since Daniel lived until at least the beginning of the return from exile, I believe it is quite possible that he knew how mightily God had responded after his time of prayer and fasting. I do hope so. What joy it would have brought to the heart of this faithful man of God! Makes me smile just thinking about it!

Daniel 9:20-27

Here we are on Day 41 in our flight toward independent reading of God's Word for devotional insights. How are you doing? Are you seeing how beautifully God speaks to us even through difficult passages of Scripture? Are you "okay" living with the tension of not understanding everything perfectly, but accepting that you'll grasp a bit more each time you read? That is my prayer for you, and that has been the story of my lifetime journey in God's Word. As I read and reread His Word slowly year after year, I find that a deeper understanding grows each time. It's like uncovering treasure. At the same time, I'm also learning to be content with the hard places, the passages I cannot understand. After all, God's ways are so much higher than my ways. I'd have to be God to comprehend Him completely (and I am definitely not!). Oh, but I know that when I nestle into His Word, God always gives me the understanding I need for that season in my life. It's thrilling to still be making discoveries in my early sixties, and if God wills, how joyful it would be to continue gleaning and discerning more, into my eighties and beyond, like our friend Daniel. The Bible is never old or boring. God gives new insights each time we come to His Word with an asking heart.

Today we return to prophecy and vision and mystery. We'll meet Gabriel again, winging his way toward Daniel. I'm amazed at the great way Daniel was honored to receive these messages about times yet to come. How strong was his faith, honed through years of faithful prayer in a hard place. He definitely deserves his place in the Hebrews Hall of Fame:

> How much more do I need to say? It would take too long to recount the stories of the faith of Gideon, Barak, Samson, Jephthah, David, Samuel, and all the prophets. By faith these people overthrew kingdoms, ruled with justice, and received what God had promised them. They shut the mouths of lions, quenched the flames of fire, and escaped death by the edge of the sword. Their weakness was turned to strength. They became strong in battle and put whole armies to flight. —Hebrews 11:32-34

How often do we have an opportunity to listen in on a conversation between a man and an angel? Wow. That awaits us as we turn to the last part of Daniel 9 and seek what God has for us today.

Father God, teach us from Your Word. Help us to grasp and understand what we need for this time, this day, this season in our lives. In Jesus' Name, Amen.

My Reflections

Request:

Read: Daniel 9:20-27

Write out your verse.

Record:

Write a response to the Lord.

Respond:

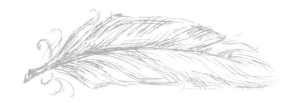

Sharon's Reflections

As Daniel continued in prayer, Gabriel arrived "at the time of the evening sacrifice." I wonder how many days Daniel had prayed and fasted? I confess to you I often pray for a very short time and then give up and move on, whether I've heard an answer or not. Perhaps my longings and aches are not as big as Daniel's were. Perhaps living in the comfort and prosperity of America has made me soft. I want to be more like Daniel, seeking God earnestly and continuing to pray, continuing to ask for the needs of my family, my friends, my church, my community, my country, the world.

I love that Gabriel assures Daniel, "The moment you began praying, a command was given. And now I am here . . ." (Daniel 9:23a). God hears when we pray. As soon as we pray! And the answer will come. I love that Daniel is reassured of this and is given further understanding of a vision. To be honest, I'm not sure what vision is being referred to here. Is it a new vision Daniel had? Is it further detail on one of the older visions? I don't know.

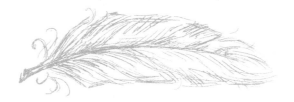

What I do know is that God clearly has all the answers. He has a plan. The days of our lives are numbered, and the days of life on planet earth before Jesus' Second Coming are also numbered. What is shrouded in mystery for us is crystal clear to God. "At the appointed time," Jesus will return. Nations will rise and fall; arrogant men will strut about and be destroyed by death, disease, or conquest. Only God and His Kingdom will remain.

Do you remember that rock from Daniel 2 in King Nebuchadnezzar's dream? It shattered all the other kingdoms and it became the foundation of the Kingdom that never ends. That's what I look forward to with eager anticipation. I say with John in Revelation, "Maranatha! Come, Lord Jesus, Come!" (Revelation 22:20, my paraphrase).

Sharon's Verse: "The moment you began praying, a command was given. And now I am here to tell you what it was, for you are very precious to God. Listen carefully so that you can understand the meaning of your vision." —Daniel 9:23

Sharon's Response: *The vision in this passage likely refers to one Daniel doesn't describe for us. Although I'm unclear about the vision, what I do see, Lord, is that You hear us the very moment we pray. I love that You sent Gabriel to Daniel because Daniel was "precious" to You. How beautiful and how like You, Father! Oh, how You love us! This telling of the end times and the hard times before the end is chilling. Yet even in this part of the story, You triumph. You have decreed a "fate for the defiler" that will be "poured out on him." You will not allow evil to triumph forever. How I thank You for that. I ask that You will give me understanding, Lord, of what I need to learn from every passage in Your Word and trust You with what I cannot understand. I thank You for Your assurance that You hear me when I pray. In Your Son's Name, Jesus, Amen.*

I had in mind to research this part of Daniel, so I could explain this vision . . . but I decided not to. My desire is to model for you what I do in my devotional reading when something seems beyond me. I ask for help. I find the treasures that I do understand, and I trust that God will show me the rest. If I have time to research, I do. If all the time I have that day is my normal space for a quiet time, I close my Bible, contented that God knows . . . and He will show me what I need to know or to do. I invite you to research what scholars have said about this vision should you wish or simply find your verse and trust Him with what you don't yet understand. Who knows? Maybe it will be revealed to us when we're in our eighties!

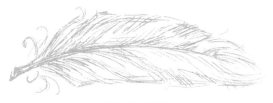

Daniel 10

As you will see from this chapter, Daniel is a man of self-discipline. His heart is God's, and he seeks to serve Him alone. He had been fasting from rich foods and not indulging in fancy oil treatments when God sends him another vision. We don't even hear a description of this vision until the next chapter. Today, we watch as Daniel encounters an angel who will interpret the vision for him. Yes, an angel!

In this amazing passage we are given a glimpse into spiritual warfare. It's fascinating to read of battles fought between angels and demons and to realize that another whole dimension exists—a spiritual dimension populated with beings that are also at war until the end comes. Paul talks about spiritual warfare in clear terms in Ephesians:

> A final word: Be strong in the Lord and in his mighty power. Put on all of God's armor so that you will be able to stand firm against all strategies of the devil. For we are not fighting against flesh-and-blood enemies, but against evil rulers and authorities of the unseen world, against mighty powers in this dark world, and against evil spirits in the heavenly places. Therefore, put on every piece of God's armor so you will be able to resist the enemy in the time of evil. Then after the battle you will still be standing firm. —Ephesians 6:10-13

We may not understand, but the spiritual realm is very real. Aren't you glad to know that angels fight for you? Aren't you glad that we are equipped for battle when we stay in God's Word and in prayer? I sure am.

Mighty God, how we praise You that You are Lord and King over all powers and principalities! Nothing has dominion over You. We rest in that as we read Your Word. Teach us Your truth. In Jesus' Name, Amen.

My Reflections

Request:

Read: Daniel 10

Write out your verse.

Record:

Write a response to the Lord.

Respond:

Sharon's Reflections

In this passage, we have one of our deepest looks at a conversation between an angelic being and a man anywhere in Scripture. When I think of the powerful energy coming from this being, I tremble a bit myself. No one but Daniel remained to meet with this angel. The men with him all ran. They ran! Think about that. Grown men, maybe men accustomed to hard times as captives in Babylon. And yet they were overcome with a sense of the surreal and "other" than human, and they fled and hid. I have a feeling I might have been a runner and a hider myself unless God had given me the strength to stay my ground. Did you see the way just seeing this angel weakened Daniel? He describes it like this: "My strength left me, my face grew deathly pale, and I felt very weak. . . . I fainted and lay there with my face to the ground. . . . I stood up, still trembling. . . . My strength is gone, and I can hardly breathe" (Daniel 10:8b, 9b, 11b, 17b).

Interestingly, one of God's amazing names is Jehovah Sabaoth, the LORD of Hosts.

God is in charge of Heaven's armies. If just one angel causes a strong man to tremble and faint, what must it be like to see all of Heaven's armies? In Matthew 26:53, Jesus tells His disciples who want to fight for Him when He's arrested, "Do you think I cannot call on my Father, and he will at once put at my disposal more than twelve legions of angels?" (NIV). I asked my history-teacher husband how many men were in a Roman legion, and he told me between five and six thousand men. If we multiply only 5,000 by twelve, Jesus was saying that He had more than 60,000 angels instantly at His command. Whoa. We'd do more than tremble if we saw that army, wouldn't we?

I'm reminded of a line from *The Lion, the Witch, and the Wardrobe* when Mr. Beaver tells the children about Aslan (who represents Christ), "He is not safe." No, our God is not safe and cozy and small and controllable. He commands legions upon legions of beings the sight of which would cause us to run in terror. He is bigger than we can imagine, mightier than we ever dreamed, and more terrifying to His enemies than we can bear to ponder. And yet . . . He is a tender Shepherd to those He has called by name. We are under His protection. We are His. And because of that, though He might not be "safe" . . . we are.

Sharon's Verse: "'Don't be afraid,' he said, 'for you are very precious to God. Peace! Be encouraged! Be strong!' . . ." (Daniel 10:19a).

Sharon's Response: *Father, this whole passage helps me realize how difficult it is for human beings to handle the mysteries of the spiritual realm without Your help and support. Yet the glimpse we are given of angels and wars with demonic forces heightens my belief in You. Thank You that Your angels bring peace, encouragement, and strength. The demonic forces delight to terrorize, but not so with Your beautiful angels. They comfort and strengthen us as they bring Your messages, calming our fears.*

If you are interested in reading about another incredible time when men were allowed to see into the spiritual realm, normally invisible to us, turn over to 2 Kings 6:8-23. There we read the amazing story of Elisha and his servant, who were surrounded by a real army sent to seize Elisha. The servant is frantic while Elisha is calm. The servant settles down considerably when Elisha prays that the servant's eyes will be opened, and he is able to see the hillsides filled with angelic horses and chariots of fire—an army at the ready and larger by far than the human army! We really do have angels watching over us. Oh, how grateful I am that I belong to the Lord of Hosts!

Daniel 11:1-24

Today's passage describes battles and wars that lay ahead beyond Daniel's life span. Charles Swindoll says this: "Daniel 11 is one of the most remarkable chapters in the entire Bible. In the first thirty-five verses, there are dozens of prophecies that by now have been literally fulfilled and confirmed by historical events." That's amazing. Just think . . . much of what Daniel was told came to pass in the exact detail in which it was described! Since the purpose of our study is devotional reading, we won't talk here about these historical specifics. However, if you are interested, I've listed two excellent resources at the end of this study for you to look into further.

As we read, instead of looking at the actual fulfillments, let's look at the endless back and forth of winners and losers. Let's observe the attitudes of those rulers. What traits do we see in them that we'd want to emulate? What traits make them evil? As you read this as a story, you will see a woman abandoned . . . a king who stirs up enmity . . . kingdoms uprooted and handed to a new conqueror . . . rage and anger . . . pride and executions . . . short-lived successes . . . violence and destruction . . . insolence and shame. Ultimately, each ruler will die. As do we all.

Honestly, if we live only for this life here and now, we are falling short of the entire picture. We were not created to live for only a short time. We were created to live forever. What an amazing thing to anticipate! Hear these words from 1 Thessalonians and be encouraged.

And now, dear brothers and sisters, we want you to know what will happen to the believers who have died so you will not grieve like people who have no hope. For since we believe that Jesus died and was raised to life again, we also believe that when Jesus returns, God will bring back with him the believers who have died. We tell you this directly from the Lord: We who are still living when the Lord returns will not meet him ahead of those who have died. For the Lord himself will come down from heaven with a commanding shout, with the voice of the archangel, and with the trumpet call of God. First, the believers who have died will rise from their graves. Then, together with them, we who are still alive and remain on the earth will be caught up in the clouds to meet the Lord in the air. Then we will be with the Lord forever. So encourage each other with these words. —1 Thessalonians 4:13-18

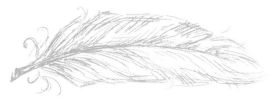

Of course, this is only an encouragement if we belong to Christ. Those rulers you are going to study now? Like all of us, they will face a final judgment. Living forever is a serious matter if you have chosen hell by your rejection of God.

Dear Wonderful Creator God, thank You for making us for eternity. Thank You that no matter how our lives turn out on earth, they are a short breath of time compared to the richness of an eternity with You. Teach us about the futility of men grasping for power in mortal bodies. In Jesus' Name, Amen.

My Reflections

Request:

Read: Daniel 11:1-24

Write out your verse.

Record:

Write a response to the Lord.

Respond:

Sharon's Reflections

Wow. What did you think about those dizzying descriptions of the rise and fall of kingdoms and men and even their wives? What stood out to you? I'd love to sit and have a good chat with you about it. I was blown away as I read the ups and the downs. It didn't seem to matter how powerful a certain king might be or how brilliant he might think his alliances were. In the end, he died. Inevitably. Every one of the humans mentioned in this first part of Daniel 11 died. Not one of them was still in charge of the kingdom they coveted so desperately.

The women mentioned also fascinated me. The daughter of the king of the south in Daniel 11:6 is given in marriage to create an alliance. Yet she loses her influence. I wonder what that means? Did her husband tire of her and look for a younger wife? How awful to be abandoned in a foreign kingdom by a husband you didn't even choose for yourself. My heart hurts for her and her lack of choice. The next alliance by marriage is mentioned in verse 17 and also failed to bring about power for the one who arranged it. Pondering these women given in marriage for political gain gave me a whole new reason to be thankful for the time and place in which we live. I'm glad I never have to stress about being a pawn in a ruler's scheme. Are we grateful for the relatively peaceful lives we currently live? Let's notice . . . the joys and blessings we do have. My complaints and whines seem awfully petty when laid against the lives of the women Daniel mentions here.

Sharon's Verse: "After the enemy army is swept away, the king of the south will be filled with pride and will execute many thousands of his enemies. But his success will be short lived." —Daniel 11:12

Sharon's Response: *It's the last sentence that hits me, Lord. In the midst of pride and brutality, this king "thinks" he's made it to the top of the heap. Yet his "success" will be short lived and will come tumbling down. I think of what Jesus said, "For what will it profit a man if he gains the whole world, and loses his own soul?" (Mark 8:36 NKJV). And, of course, even if a man did gain the entire world, it would be temporary, because men are mortal: they live; they die; they face judgment. Help me, Lord, to live in light of eternity. Help me to remember that all on this earth is temporary. I hold to Your everlasting and always faithful Hand.*

I wonder what is happening in the world as you do this study, dear reader. Is the world in the middle of a seismic pandemic as it was when I was writing this? Are wars going on in Asia or Africa or even in America? Have frightening dictators come to power in some part of the world? Whatever scary event might be happening, think of the kings described here in Daniel and remember what happened to them. Oh, dear one, if you are His . . . it ends well for you. Rejoice in that and pray for those who suffer in the here and now.

Resources for further study:
bible.org/seriespage/11-world-history-darius-time-end
blueletterbible.org/Comm/archives/guzik_david/StudyGuide_Dan/Dan_11.cfm

Daniel 11:25-45

As you continue to read this great tale of the rise and fall of kingdoms, continue looking for themes. Watch for family troubles. Consider what the lust for riches and treasures do to the greedy. Ponder the hatred spewed toward God's people. Ask yourself what has actually changed in all these centuries. It's amazing really how much people are still the same today. Still those among us hungry for land and possessions. Still men hurting others to get what they want. Still Jews persecuted around the globe. Still many families troubled and not the source of joy they were meant to be. Wars, intrigue, and political fighting remain to this day.

What is one small person like you or me to do in the midst of all this turmoil? Our job is simply to follow Christ right where we are. No matter our situation, we are called to surrender to the Spirit who lives within us. We are to bear fruit, and God tells us just what that fruit looks like: "love, joy, peace, patience, kindness, goodness, faithfulness, gentleness and self-control" (Galatians 5:22-23). Wherever we find ourselves, we can live out these qualities. We can help our neighbors with love and care. We can spread the word that God exists, He's there, He's good, and He will one day return as Judge and King. Yes, we can do much in our own sphere of influence, even if we aren't one of those ruling types. (And if we are, we had best rule well, surrendering to the one true God in all we do and say.)

Watch also as you read for little pieces of encouragement, hope, and confidence along the way. Seek and you will find them. Notice how we are reminded about God's "appointed time" and "the end of all things." God holds all this mess that is our broken world in His perfect hands, and He will bring good and order and peace in His appointed time.

Oh, Father, as we near the end of the book of Daniel, give us eyes to see and ears to hear what You would teach us. We look to You in awe that You are able to speak to us through Your Word. In Jesus' Name we read in expectation. Amen.

My Reflections

Request:

Read: Daniel 11:25-45

Write out your verse.

Record:

Write a response to the Lord.

Respond:

Sharon's Reflections

I feel confident that God met you in your reading. With so many rich nuggets in this passage, I suspect each of us found one to examine and ponder as we mined for them with the Holy Spirit as our guide. Although I didn't pick verse 27 for my personal devotional choice today, I'd like to look at it together and see what we can learn from this verse: "Seeking nothing but each other's harm, these kings will plot against each other at the conference table, attempting to deceive each other. But it will make no difference, for the end will come at the appointed time" (Daniel 11:27).

Seeking nothing but each other's harm. How very sad that these kings looked only for ways to harm others at that table. No matter how appealing a gathering might look on the outside, no matter how promising it seems to see various powers and rulers gathered,

only the heart really matters. If the heart is evil, any promises made are flimsy and untrustworthy.

These kings will plot against each other. Isn't it dreadful that, as they sit around this conference table, they are plotting internally and intentionally to deceive? Oh, let's be wise ourselves when we deal with people of bad intent. Wicked hearts are bent on deception. It should not shock us, but we need to be wary.

It will make no difference, for the end will come at the appointed time. Here's the punch line. And we smile. What a grand way for God to tell us not to fret. All these deceptions and intrigues? In the end, Jesus will return at the appointed time, and no king or ruler will be able to stand against Him. I think about small children making plans to build a fort. No matter how much they work at it and want to stay there, if the parents come out to their play area and tell them to come in for a nap, in they will come, either obediently or hauled bodily away. Right? God wins. Every time.

Sharon's Verse: "He will flatter and win over those who have violated the covenant. But the people who know their God will be strong and will resist him." —Daniel 11:32

Sharon's Response: *Father, it boils down to this. We need to know You. It's those who know You that are able to resist the flattery and the lies and the deceptions of the enemy. Help me, Lord, to know You more and more so I am not deceived, so that I can be strong and resist all who would come against what is good and holy and right.*

I haven't mentioned Sweet Selah Ministries in this book, but the motto of the ministry I founded in 2017 is "Taking time to know God and love Him more and more." That thought fits perfectly with my verse for today. I suspect that might be exactly why I was drawn to it.

Dear one, a time may come when to worship Jesus openly is a crime. A time may come when you and I will be put to the test and challenged to violate what we know is right. There is only one way to be strong and resist and that is to know God so well that we lean in when it gets tough and draw strength from Him. You are gaining that strength with every reading, every writing, every day invested in studying His Word to know Him better. And in knowing God, you can't help but grow to love Him more and more.

I'm grateful that you are reading along with me. There is no greater study on earth than the study of God and who He is. Our very lives ultimately depend on knowing Him. Our God is good. Our God is love. Our God is with us. Always. Come what may.

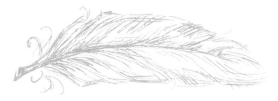

Daniel 12

Here we are at the very end of this small, exciting, mysterious, challenging book. You did it! You've met with God each day as we've studied Daniel together. You've puzzled over some of the passages, struggled to choose a verse on occasion, and had flashes of deep insight and application. At least, that's my prayer for you. Most of all, I hope you've seen that even a short time spent in God's Word is rich in learning and growth when you come with the focus that the 4Rs bring to the task. Today, we finish the explanation of Daniel's last recorded vision and hear about the very end times.

This chapter is filled with hope. In verse 2 you'll read about the Book of Life, a great book in which is written the name of every child of God. We read more about this book in Revelation when the New Jerusalem is described. "Nothing evil will be allowed to enter, nor anyone who practices shameful idolatry and dishonesty—but only those whose names are written in the Lamb's Book of Life" (Revelation 21:27). Paul also mentions this book in Philippians when he's discussing a quarrel between two ladies, asking members of the Philippian church to help them. "And I ask you, my true partner, to help these two women, for they worked hard with me in telling others the Good News. They worked along with Clement and the rest of my co-workers, whose names are written in the Book of Life" (Philippians 4:3).

This chapter will remind you that, if you belong to Him, one day you will "shine like the stars forever" (vs. 3). And So Much More! The second coming of Jesus, described in Daniel 12, will bring great joy to those who know Him and great terror to those who refuse to acknowledge Him. Daniel makes this very clear. Oh, friend, do you know Him? Is *your* name in the Book of Life? If you have any doubts at all, I would like to share with you how simple it is to turn to the One who loves you and wants you with Him in Heaven forever. See page 15 for help in receiving Jesus as Savior. It is my prayer that no one reads this little book, *Give Me Wings to Soar*, without knowing the One under whose wings we can safely rest! My longing is to see each reader know the shelter of the Almighty and learn to fly on eagle's wings, even when the storms come, because they know the one true God.

How thankful we are, dear Lord, that You record the names of Your children. Not one of us who belongs to You will be lost. Thank You, Father, that we are safe in Your hands.

Teach us as we finish this great book of Daniel. We come ready to hear and yearning to know. In Jesus' Name, Amen.

My Reflections

Request:

Read: Daniel 12

Write out your verse.

Record:

Write a response to the Lord.

Respond:

Sharon's Reflections

I have found it very insightful when I reach the end of a Bible book study with this method to go back and review the verses I chose one last time. I often find patterns and repetitions of what the Lord has shown me. This time through Daniel, I felt the deep reassurance that I do not need to fear any earthly ruler. I must simply keep my eyes on my Heavenly Father. How about you? Has God opened your eyes to His truth in a specific way throughout your readings?

Here are some lessons we can glean from the book as a whole:

Stay small and let God be big. Seriously, all those rulers puffed up with pride? It didn't go well for them. There was the great Nebuchadnezzar grazing in the field and eating grass. Don't forget Belshazzar, feasting and carousing the night, his city was invaded. The night he was killed! And all the kings and kingdoms in the dreams and visions toppled. We are not big. God is.

Prayer matters to God and to us. Daniel's prayers have taught us much about how to pray. Through Daniel's steady habit of praying three times a day facing Jerusalem God gave him miraculous success. He asked for God's help in interpreting Nebuchadnezzar's dream. He prayed for help understanding visions. Daniel came to God consistently . . . All The Time . . . because he knew God and loved Him. God clearly told Daniel that his prayers were heard and, in fact, angels were dispatched to answer them! Prayer matters to God. And prayer matters to us.

Follow God's rules at all times. From the moment the teenager Daniel refused the rich foods of the king, we watched him follow God's commands. He was faithful even when it sure seemed like he had been deserted. He and his friends kept true to the one God to the point of threatened death . . . by fire and then by ravenous lions. They simply did the right thing no matter what. And their lives were fruitful even as captives in a foreign land.

In the end, God wins. Throughout the book of Daniel, we are assured of this over and over, but my very favorite reassurance was in Nebuchadnezzar's dream. I'll end with that after I share my verse with you.

Sharon's Verse: "As for you, go your way until the end. You will rest, and then at the end of the days, you will rise again to receive the inheritance set aside for you." —Daniel 12:13

Sharon's Response: *Simple instructions for Daniel: Keep going, as you have been, faithful in prayer and duty. Father, keep me faithful in prayer and duty as well. I love the promise of rest and resurrection for Daniel. He will be alive and very well at the end of days. All of us who are God's children will be alive and very well. And a rich inheritance awaits us. Thank You, Lord, that despite the violence of man and the wickedness of wars and persecutions on this planet, the end for us is just the beginning.*

Be encouraged, dear one, as you read these words God gave Daniel as we close this amazing book:

"During the reigns of those kings, the God of heaven will set up a kingdom that will never be destroyed or conquered. It will crush all these kingdoms into nothingness, and it will stand forever. That is the meaning of the rock cut from the mountain, though not by human hands, that crushed to pieces the statue of iron, bronze, clay, silver, and gold. The great God was showing the king what will happen in the future. The dream is true, and its meaning is certain." —Daniel 2:44-45

193

Psalm 3

Do you get excited like I do when a singer comes on the radio and explains why he wrote one of your favorite songs? I love hearing the backstory. It makes the lyrics even more meaningful, and I love learning the stories of hymns too. Knowing that Horatio Spafford wrote "It is Well with My Soul" after the deaths of all four of his children makes my eyes swim in tears whenever I sing that magnificent hymn.

Today, as we look at Psalm 3, we actually hear a backstory. My Bible describes it this way: "A psalm of David, regarding the time David fled from his son Absalom." You can read this sad tale in full in 2 Samuel 15-18. Absalom had decided to win the people away from his father, King David, and take the throne from him. Ow! Can you imagine the hurt, the pain, the wounding that caused David? Betrayed by his own son. Keep this context in mind as you read this psalm, and may God guide you to the verse He wants you to focus on today.

Dear Lord, we can't fully imagine the pain King David must have felt as he wrote this song to You. As we read, help us to discern what You have to teach us from this passage of Your Word. Give us attention and focus. We want to hear from You. In Jesus' Name, Amen.

My Reflections

Request:

Read: Psalm 3

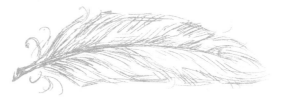

Write out your verse.

Record:

Write a response to the Lord.

Respond:

Sharon's Reflections

Psalm 3 uses "our" word *Selah* (translated as *Interlude* in the *New Living Translation*). David writes a thought and then asks us to pause and ponder before we move on. In the first two verses, he lays out his problem before the Lord. That's the perfect place to begin when we are distressed and hurting, isn't it? We can run to God and simply pour out to Him our hurts, our disappointments, our pain. David has two complaints. First, he's facing a lot of enemies. In fact, Absalom was so successful that his rebellion had drawn a sizable army to his side. David, with his own army and all his wives, has been forced to

flee, leaving Jerusalem to seek refuge out in the wilderness. Second, David is disturbed by the widespread belief that the situation is hopeless. The people were saying, "God will never rescue him!" (Psalm 3:2b).

Right after the complaint, David's second stanza in this psalm-song is all about praising God. He declares the truth that God is His shield, His glory, and the One who lifts His head high. He affirms the truth that when he cries out to God, God does indeed answer. I love the triumph he expresses, refuting all the words the naysayers were drilling into his mind. David fought those negative thoughts with the truth of Who God Is. I want to do the same when doubt and discouraging thoughts threaten to overwhelm me.

The last section of this beautiful outcry to God is an amazing expression of trust. David is able to lie down and sleep even though a huge army is racing to kill him and his family. He asks God to fight for him—and even gives God suggestions about the way He should treat his enemies. He ends with a triumphant declaration: "Victory comes from you, O Lord . . ." (Psalm 3:8a).

Every time I read a psalm, I learn more about how to approach God in prayer and worship and petition. I need frequent reminders, because those negative thoughts can scream pretty loudly at times. That's another reason we read the Word of God each day. Just like I need to eat and give my body good nutritious substances every day, I need daily filling of good spiritual nutrition. I believe you agree with me and that's why we're on this journey in His Word together. How thankful I am for that.

Sharon's Verse: "Arise, O Lord! Rescue me, my God! Slap all my enemies in the face! Shatter the teeth of the wicked!" —Psalm 3:7

Sharon's Response: *So much passion here, Lord. David cries out to You in great sorrow and grief. He doesn't say, "Help me fight well." He asks You to fight. Is this because his enemy is his own son, Lord? Is that why his request regarding his enemies is on the mild side? It's almost a "shake some sense into him" thought. It's always encouraging to see the way David turns to You in every situation. His trust in You inspires me. Help me to always trust and turn to You like that as well.*

I'd love to close out our time together with a prayer taken directly from Psalm 3:8: *Father God, we declare with David, "Victory comes from You." Help us to let go of striving to solve our problems on our own. Keep us running to You. Please bless Your people today. Especially, Lord, bless those reading this book. Thank You. In Jesus' Name, Amen.*

Proverbs 3

In the distant past, I used to grumble about all those handicapped parking places in restaurant lots. Frequently, they sat empty while the lot was full, and I would have to drive my able-bodied self to the far reaches to find a parking space. I wondered why they needed four spots when no one was even utilizing them. I'm not proud of this attitude. I'm just being honest here.

But then my father-in-law moved in with us. Because he was totally wheelchair bound, we purchased a handicapped van for him, and not only did we need a handicapped parking spot, we needed a van-accessible spot. When we couldn't find one, we needed two handicapped spaces to safely unload him. All of a sudden, my understanding changed. [Sigh.] Eating out was one of his great joys and one of the few pleasures he had left. It was such a disappointment when we couldn't find available parking. That's what it took for me to value those precious spots for those who need them. I'm ashamed to confess my former inaccurate understanding. As you read Proverbs 3, you will come across its most famous verse, Proverbs 3:5. We are to trust God and not our own inaccurate understanding. What a great theme for our lives.

Dear Lord, we seek Your will as we read. Help us not to rely on ourselves but look to You. Underline for us the verse of your choosing today. In Jesus' Name, Amen.

My Reflections

Request:

Read: Proverbs 3

Write out your verse.

Record:

Write a response to the Lord.

Respond:

Sharon's Reflections

I love all the good advice in Proverbs 3. I love that following this advice will give us full and satisfying lives. I want to trust God with "all my heart." And yet, despite that desire . . . how often I fail! We all do, right? Sometimes we have a tendency to read these words of wisdom with a sinking feeling, realizing how far we are from actually doing the good things Solomon teaches us. But let's not go there.

We need to approach these clearly-expressed truths with teachable hearts and with an awareness that growing in righteousness is a slow process. When I was young, my temper was fierce and hot and quick. It has taken decades for me to reach a point where I'm very seldom angry—after thousands of failures along the way. Even now, I know the damage I'm capable of inflicting with my tongue. I'm thankful that God never gave up on me as I continued to come back to Him with my need to let go of outrage and remain calm and gentle over disappointments in life. Time after time, I went back to Him, and each time I grew a teensy bit better at maintaining my cool.

If you feel inadequate as you read, don't be discouraged, friend. We all do. Being shaped and refined into Christ-likeness is the work of a lifetime. *The stumbling is humbling.* Every failure to live up to the best standards simply reminds us yet again of our great need for a loving and forgiving Savior. We run to Him and find cleansing and love and grace in abundance—and this gives us love and grace to share with others. All along the way, slowly but surely, we look more and more like Jesus. Praise God!

Sharon's Verse: "Never let loyalty and kindness leave you! Tie them around your neck as a reminder. Write them deep within your heart." —Proverbs 3:3

Sharon's Response: *I love these two traits linked together—loyalty and kindness. Help me to "write them deep within my heart." Loyalty matters. Help me to keep my word, to be there for others, to defend a friend's reputation even when they're not around. Help me to be known as a caring person, a person of kindness, not given to rage or spite or contrariness. Keep me loyal. Make me kind. I love the results described in the very next verse: "Then you will find favor with both God and people, and you will earn a good reputation" (vs. 4). Thank You, Lord, for the wisdom in Proverbs. Help me to not just read, but to do what You say.*

Tomorrow, we move to the New Testament and begin a book with a different format and style of biblical writing. You are getting very close to the time when you will (hopefully) thank me kindly for the lessons and then just up and soar away, ready to dig into any book of the Bible and have a meaningful study on your own with just God and you.

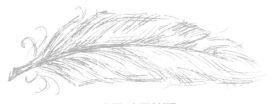

Colossians 1:1-14

Today, we leave the Old Testament and begin a study in the New Testament book of Colossians. You'll notice that the format is changing as you move closer to an independent Bible study without notes from me. First, our prayer together before you embark on the 4Rs is missing. My desire is for you to pray—just you—to the God who hears. Also, I've buried the verse I chose and my responses in a general section called "Sharon's Notes." These notes are for you if you're interested, but I want your main focus to be on all that God speaks to your heart during your reading of His Word.

Other changes greet us as we begin to study a new book in the Bible. While Daniel is a book of history and prophecy, Colossians is a letter penned by the apostle Paul with much love and passion to a new church.

Paul was one of the greatest missionaries of all time and an amazing follower of the Lord Jesus Christ. You can read the story of his incredible adventures in the book of Acts. There we first meet him as a persecutor of Christians, a man zealous for his faith in God alone, but lacking understanding that Jesus was the Messiah he had been waiting for. That all changed one day when Jesus Himself appeared and spoke to Paul, blinding him with the glory of His Presence.

Once Paul realized Jesus was Messiah, he was all in—heart and soul—and dedicated the rest of his life to sharing the good news of Christ's life and death and resurrection. It's an amazing story of a remarkable man devoted to the Lord. When Paul wrote the letter to the Colossians, his life was nearing an end. He wrote from prison to the Christians who met together in the city of Colossae. Keep in mind as you read that Paul was suffering for his faith and no longer a free man able to go wherever he wished. Yet his heart is for this beloved church of believers and his focus is on Jesus and on their walk with Him . . . not on his own suffering in prison.

In Daniel, we watched a young Jewish man hold on to his God and his faith in a foreign culture that worshiped other gods. In Colossians we'll watch Paul redirect a church that did not rightly understand who Jesus was—God in flesh. You see, we can be pulled away from God's truth not only by our culture (like the one surrounding Daniel), but also by those who twist and misinterpret God's Word (heresy within the church). I think it's important for us to be aware of this. Colossians is a great book that calls us back to sound beliefs.

In addition, Paul gives marvelous and practical advice on living out the Christian life day by day. You're going to love that part of the book as well.

Paul never visited Colossae, which is located in modern day Turkey. He did, however, visit and minister in a nearby town called Ephesus. Paul visited Ephesus briefly during his second missionary journey (see Acts 18:19-21) and then returned for over two years on his third missionary journey (see Acts 19 – Acts 20:1). A man named Epaphras, who came to know Christ through Paul's teaching in Ephesus, traveled to Colossae to share the Good News. His message was received by many there and a church was established.

Epaphras later left home and traveled to Rome to serve Paul in prison. He brought news of the fellowship at Colossae and shared with Paul that the church was embracing a heresy that Christ was not God in the flesh. Paul wrote this letter in love to them, calling them back to this core belief and writing some of the finest words ever written about the supremacy of the Lord Jesus Christ. Just wait until you read it. It's magnificent!

With this bit of background, are you ready for this next stage in your flight toward solo Bible study? You are definitely advanced in Flight lessons at this point, and I'm praying for each reader that you will be readied by this book to soar. Let's dive into the Scripture.

My Reflections

Request:

Read: Colossians 1:1-14

Record:

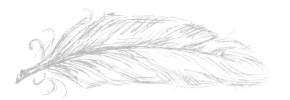

Respond:

Sharon's notes:

I chose the verse, "This same Good News that came to you is going out all over the world. It is bearing fruit everywhere by changing lives, just as it changed your lives from the day you first heard and understood the truth about God's wonderful grace" (Colossians 1:6). I was simply overwhelmed by the fact that this same Good News is preached today. Isn't that amazing? And it still bears fruit by changing lives.

Oh, Lord, what a marvel that Your truth is as life changing today as it was in Paul's day! How I thank You for Your wonderful grace that enables me to live above the storms of life—and for the sure hope of life everlasting. I share with Paul the "confident hope of what God has reserved for [me] in heaven" (vs. 5). It makes all the difference in the way I live today, Lord, knowing life everlasting is ahead of me.

I hope God met you in a special way as you read His Word. I pray that this letter to the Colossians will teach you how to discern truth from error. I pray that He blesses you with insights and "aha!" moments that shape the way you live out your days. I pray that you come to know Him better and love Him more and more as you listen to Him speak through His living Word lovingly written by His servant Paul.

DAY 49 FLIGHT

Colossians 1:15-22

This is one of the most glorious passages in Scripture in my opinion. It's majestic and lyrical and full of the highest praise for the only One worthy of our worship. If you can, read it out loud. Or at least read in a whisper. Let the words that honor and describe Him fill your heart and mind.

My Reflections

Request:

Read: Colossians 1:15-22

Record:

Respond:

Sharon's notes:

I suspect you've tried to remove a stain from a garment. Who hasn't inadvertently spilled tomato sauce or mustard or some other atrocious substance all over a shirt or pants or dress? It's not fun getting it out. You try to remember whether to use hot water or cold.

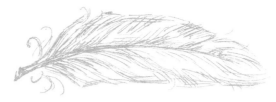

You search for a spray bottle of spot remover. You scrub and let it soak and finally wash it with trepidation, hoping it will somehow come clean. If you're like me, a small remainder is often left behind, a shadow of that stain. Definitely not "brand new clean" anymore. It's discouraging. (That's one reason I don't buy high-end clothing. Why bother when they will tear and stain just as easily as the more reasonably priced items?)

So . . . why am I talking about stains on clothing? It ties in to the verse I chose from today's reading. I could have chosen any one of those verses and probably have in the past when I've read Colossians before. I love every single word and sentence in Paul's tribute and description of Jesus. But today what struck me was all that Jesus accomplished for us. In fact, it took my breath away. "Yet now he has reconciled you to himself through the death of Christ in his physical body. As a result, he has brought you into his own presence, and you are holy and blameless as you stand before him without a single fault" (Colossians 1:22).

My God and my King! What is this You have done? Reconciled. Clean. All sin gone. Nothing left sticking to me and stinking. Jesus' death was totally sufficient. And I stand before You in trembling awe—holy, blameless, without a single fault—how can this be? And yet it is. And therefore I fall to my knees and adore You.

I hope you too are walking away from our study in awe of the person of Jesus Christ, the "visible image of the invisible God." Paul had an encounter with Christ that changed him forever. He was literally blinded. When Paul tells us who Jesus is, he's talking from intimate, personal, up-close knowledge. In fact, as well as that first experience with Christ, Paul had others. In 2 Corinthians, Paul tries to explain the inexplicable: ". . . I will reluctantly tell about visions and revelations from the Lord. I was caught up to the third heaven fourteen years ago. Whether I was in my body or out of my body, I don't know. . . . But I do know that I was caught up to paradise and heard things so astounding that they cannot be expressed in words, things no human is allowed to tell" (2 Corinthians 12:1-4). We absolutely know God's Word is true. And Paul, who writes through the inspiration of the Holy Spirit, tells of divine encounters with God and astounding sights. When he tells us who Christ is, we can believe it wholeheartedly. If you have time, go back and read this passage one last time and linger once more in awe as you ponder the God who made Himself known through Christ Jesus, Son of God, and Son of Man.

May God whisper special and inspiring words to you; may He pour out His blessing upon you; and may these beautiful verses stay with you all day long.

Colossians 1:23-29

As we close out chapter one, notice that Paul addresses his main purpose in writing to this fledgling church. He's concerned that they are not seeing Christ accurately. He urges them not to "drift away" from what they believe. Good words for us as well. Let's stay true to what the Bible says and not allow winsome words to lure us from His truth found within the pages of Scripture.

My Reflections

Request:

Read: Colossians 1:23-29

Record:

Respond:

Sharon's notes:

Did you notice how personal Paul gets in these verses? He opened the letter with a beautiful prayer and words of encouragement and thanksgiving. Then, he turned to that glorious doctrinal description of Christ we studied yesterday. In today's passage he returns to a more personal style of writing. You catch a glimpse of his suffering and his sacrificial attitude. You hear his passion for these new Christians who serve Jesus and his longing that they be accurate in their faith, fully devoted to the Lord Jesus. He unveils secrets and highlights the beauty of a gospel meant for all people—not just for the Jewish people from whom Messiah came.

As I read these verses, God led me to meditate on the concept that Christ *lives in me*. I remember as a child not being able to comprehend that at all. How exactly could Jesus "come into my heart"? My parents helped me understand that God is Spirit, and when I invited Him into my heart, that is how I was born again into God's family—and the Holy Spirit entered me. As I grew in understanding, I also began noticing His still small voice within. I heard His directions, I felt His love, and I felt safe knowing He was right there with me.

Here's my verse and response: "For God wanted them to know that the riches and glory of Christ are for you Gentiles, too. And this is the secret: Christ lives in you. This gives you assurance of sharing his glory" (Colossians 1:27).

What a secret! You live in me. Your Spirit speaks to me and moves me from within. No force in the sky above or the earth below can keep me from Your Presence—for we are together—my body Your temple, my heart Your home. This is a mystery, Lord. How I thank You for entering in and making me new and fully Yours.

Here are some other verses to contemplate, if you wish, about what it means to have the Spirit within us. It truly is a mystery. I don't claim to understand it. Yet, what a marvel to puzzle over and attempt to grasp. No matter our age or stage there is always more to consider and learn. We will never plumb the depths of His rich Word.

And I will ask the Father, and he will give you another Advocate, who will never leave you. He is the Holy Spirit, who leads into all truth. The world cannot receive him, because it isn't looking for him and doesn't recognize him. But you know him, because he lives with you now and later will be in you. —John 14:16-17

Don't you realize that your body is the temple of the Holy Spirit, who lives in you and was given to you by God? You do not belong to yourself. —1 Corinthians 6:19

Through the power of the Holy Spirit who lives within us, carefully guard the precious truth that has been entrusted to you. —2 Timothy 1:14

May God move in you today, dear reader. If you have received Him into your heart, accepting Him as Lord and Savior, He is there with you and in you always. Listen to His voice. Ask Him to make you attentive. Go about your daily tasks rejoicing that you are not alone. You are part of this amazing mystery . . . *Christ lives in you.*

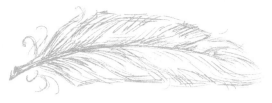

Colossians 2:1-10

As you open your Bible to the second chapter in Colossians, notice the second verse. This verse just might be the key to understanding the whole book, and it's my prayer for us today. We'll take a deeper look at this verse after you meet with God yourself.

My Reflections

Request:

Read: Colossians 2:1-10

Record:

Respond:

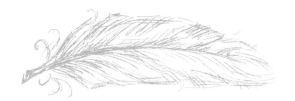

Sharon's notes:

I pray that God spoke to you through His Word giving you a rich time. Verse two, where Paul reveals his goal in writing, is worth an extra look. "My goal is that they may be encouraged in heart and united in love, so that they may have the full riches of complete understanding, in order that they may know the mystery of God, namely, Christ" (Colossians 2:2 NIV).

First, Paul has a goal in writing and a specific audience in mind. It's broader than just the Christians in the city of Colossae, but actually incorporates . . . you and me.

He writes in verse 1, "I want you to know how hard I am contending for you and for those at Laodicea, *and for all who have not met me personally*" (emphasis mine). His objective is to include those who have never heard him speak, never seen the fire and tenderness in his eyes, never been able to ask the questions burning on their hearts. That's his audience. And that includes us. Wow.

Second, his desire is that we "may be encouraged in heart and united in love." He knows better than most that we all go through difficult times. That hasn't changed all that much over the centuries. Hard times have always afflicted us as individuals and as nations. Poverty, instability, plague, wars, and natural disasters haunt and hunt us all. So, our hearts need to be encouraged. And . . . as Christians . . . we must be united in love so we can stand strong even in trying circumstances—and give hope to others.

Third, Paul's further desire is that we have "the full riches of complete understanding." Wow. Now, that's a tall order, and I'm definitely a work in progress when it comes to complete understanding. I am wonderfully grateful, though, that we have Paul's preserved letters that continue to help us and encourage us and guide us.

Fourth, and here is the crux of the matter: "in order that they may know the mystery of God, namely, Christ." Oh, let's keep that in mind as we study this letter. Who is Christ? Are we cognizant of how He represents all the fullness of the Godhead in His Person? Let's examine Paul's words carefully and know our Savior better as we read.

The verse I chose: "Let your roots grow down into him, and let your lives be built on him. Then your faith will grow strong in the truth you were taught, and you will overflow with thankfulness" (vs. 7).

Father God, I'm struck here with the result of going deep with Christ, with making sure I'm rooted in Jesus, with Him as my foundation, with a life built on Him . . . the result of this determination is . . . an overflow of Thankfulness. I am filled with joy! To know Jesus better is so grand and so wonderful that the result is a heart full of gratitude. In Heaven or on earth is no greater Master, no greater Yoke-fellow, no greater Friend, no greater Companion than Jesus, Lover of my Soul. Oh, Lord, I truly am overflowing with thankfulness at this thought.

My heart's desire is that you are also experiencing this profound sense of joy. When we go deep with Him, when our roots are drilled into the soil of His living and active Word, we can't help but overflow with a grateful, delighted heart.

I'm grateful for you. Look at you! You've read a ton of pages in this devotional, and yet here you are. Still soaking up His Word and learning with me. Thanks.

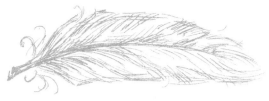

Colossians 2:11-23

When we started the second chapter of Colossians, we learned about Paul's goal for us and for all those who never had a chance to meet him face to face. (Side note: Aren't you glad we'll have an opportunity in Heaven to meet Paul personally and so many other followers of Christ!) Today, we'll uncover the heresies that were pulling the church at Colossae away from the true gospel. Watch for this as you read, and, as always, request God's help in hearing His word to you.

My Reflections

Request:

Read: Colossians 2:11-23

Record:

Respond:

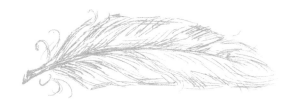

Sharon's notes:

I decided to make a list of some of the heretical teachings that had made their way into the church at Colossae. I wanted to examine them to see if I might be guilty of any of them in any way. Here's what I discovered.

Rituals. Watch out for them. If we aren't careful, they can become our religion and our focus instead of Jesus Christ. "So don't let anyone condemn you for what you eat or drink, or for not celebrating certain holy days or new moon ceremonies or Sabbaths. For these rules are only shadows of the reality yet to come . . ." (Colossians 2:16-17a).

Pious self-denial. Although denying ourselves to follow Christ is a good thing, a "showy" self-denial in an effort to earn our way to Heaven is not. That's foolish and prideful. Christ is the only One who can give us Heaven, and He offers salvation as a free gift. "Don't let anyone condemn you by insisting on pious self-denial . . ." (Colossians 2:18a).

Visions. Watch out if someone tells you they've had visions that we should worship angels—or any being—other than Christ our Lord. That is not a word from God, who makes it crystal clear that He alone is worthy of worship. We can be manipulated when someone tells us they have "heard from God." We need to remember that God does not change. Therefore, if anyone "hears" a message that does not align with Scripture, we must not listen. "Don't let anyone condemn you by insisting . . . on the worship of angels, saying they have had visions about these things. Their sinful minds have made them proud, and they are not connected to Christ, the head of the body . . ." (Colossians 2:18-19a).

Fads. We are warned to guard against any fad that tells us to focus and center on a regimen or a set of ideas and rules that are not based on Scripture. They might be fad diets, fad exercise programs, or any other trend that might be all the rage. Even good things like eating well and exercising wisely can become idols if we elevate them above our priority time with God and a life centered on hearing from Him. ". . . So why do you keep on following the rules of the world, such as, 'Don't handle! Don't taste! Don't touch!'? Such rules are mere human teachings about things that deteriorate as we use them" (Colossians 2:20b-22).

Nothing and no one should ever remove our eyes from being fixed on the Lord Jesus and His directions for our lives. Oh, how we need to be reminded of this! Here's the verse I was drawn to today: "And they [the sinful] are not connected to Christ, the head of the body. For he holds the whole body together with its joints and ligaments, and it grows as God nourishes it" (Colossians 2:19). As I pondered, I wrote to the Lord:

I love this analogy, Father. Our bones and organs are not enough on their own. We have joints and ligaments throughout that hold our bodies together and allow us to move. In the same way, if Christians are all parts of the body of Christ with different functions, and we are, then we need to be connected to Christ, the head of the body, who keeps all the ligaments and joints linked so we can move and grow and be nourished. Dear Lord Jesus, hold me close to You. Help me not to put anything in Your place as head of the body and head over my life. Help me to move for Your glory.

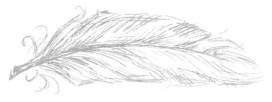

Colossians 3:1-11

So far in his letter, Paul has emphasized who Christ is: God in human form. He has warned against heresies and practices that elevate angels or visions or systems ahead of Jesus Christ Himself. Now in Colossians 3, Paul turns to good advice for these beloved Christians. Verse 1 sets the tone for the chapter: "Since you have been raised to new life with Christ . . ." (vs. 1a). Keep that phrase in mind as one born again and living in new life as a Christ follower; then study the directions Paul gives.

My Reflections

Request:

Read: Colossians 3:1-11

Record:

Respond:

Sharon's notes:

This first part of the chapter is a reminder that we are made anew when we accept Christ. Think of a butterfly tightly encased in its chrysalis. Formerly a fat and hungry caterpillar that ate itself into a deep sleep and encased itself. (Side note: that in itself is just miraculous, isn't it? How did God imagine so many vast and marvelous creatures? Only God could do that. I just can't fathom the belief that caterpillars to butterflies happened by random, natural chance and years of mutations. Just saying.) Okay. Back to the butterfly. In order to enjoy its new life, even after it has transformed within that chrysalis, our butterfly has to break out of its old home, shed that thick casing, and dry out its wings in the sunlight. Only then can it flit about among the flowers.

In the same way, when we accept Christ as our Savior, we enter a brand new state of being. God the Holy Spirit—at our request—enters into us and takes up residence within. We are totally new. However, some shedding is needed to wiggle out of our old and stiffly encased life of enslavement to sin. Paul encourages us to put off old things before we put on our pretty spectacular new clothing, our new nature—and like the butterfly, start to move our beautiful wings.

What are we to "put off"? As we review the list again, let's ask God the Holy Spirit who lives within us to reveal if any of these "old things" are still clinging to us: sexual immorality, impurity, lust, evil desires, greed, idolatry, anger, rage, malicious behavior, slander, dirty language, and lying. Oh, that's quite the list. *Father, help us to truly shed and put off these horrid remnants of an old way of living apart from You and Your grace.*

Paul then goes on to urge the Colossians to "put on" the new nature. He longs to see them renewed inside and out and rejoices that all are equal in the body of Christ, all children of the living God. No power structures exist in God's Kingdom, but we are all under Christ. In fact, the leaders are to be "servants of all."

(We'll see how important this reminder is when we study the little book of Philemon next. Paul will be reconciling a slave and a master from Colossae. He establishes this principal church-wide before he addresses it personally in his letter to Philemon, a member of the Colossian church and a slave owner.)

I focused in on verse 10 as I read: "Put on your new nature, and be renewed as you learn to know your Creator and become like him." This inspired my response:

Renew me, Lord. I want to know You more, my Creator. You chose me. You formed me. You intricately designed my DNA. Lord Jesus, You "get" me better than I do. Help me, Lord, to be all You created me to be and that involves becoming more like You. Please be in charge. Make me like You and yet still "me," a unique creation reflecting Your glory and always pointing to You.

Colossians 3:12-17

Returning to our analogy of the butterfly emerging from its chrysalis, this absolutely brilliant section of Scripture is what a Christian should look like in full flight. When we're living in the new nature, these verses will be an accurate description of us. You'll love Paul's analogy of putting on clothing. We definitely dress in different ways for different occasions, don't we? If you see me wearing old jeans, boots, and a sweatshirt, you can be pretty sure I'm not on my way to a wedding, right? Quite often, our clothing identifies who we are and what we do. As you read, ask God to help you every day to "put on" the clothing of a Christ follower.

My Reflections

Request:

Read: Colossians 3:12-17

Record:

Respond:

Sharon's notes:

Reading these insightful verses makes me want to write them out on 3 x 5 cards and memorize them. All six of them. How I would love to always be seen "dressed" as these verses describe! We are not told to dress all fancy and regal, but we are instructed that our Christian clothing ought to show Christ's love in all its glorious manifestations. Here is Paul's "wardrobe" list from that perspective.

Tenderhearted mercy: *Father, keep me from a toughened and cynical heart. It's much easier to be leery of the homeless person begging or the strange neighbor down the street than it is for me to show them mercy. Keep me wise and discerning, but also keep my heart tender and merciful.*

Kindness: *Please help me to go beyond neutrality here. I don't want to be simply "not rude." I want to actively seek to be kind, noticing the needs of others and helping as I can.*

Humility: *In pride, I often excuse my sins, puffing myself up with "understanding my story" about why I slipped, and therefore I'm somehow different from other people who slip in similar ways. Help me to acknowledge that sin is sin in my life—and help me to walk in humility, giving grace to others who have stories of their own. Forgive me when I judge myself less harshly than I judge others.*

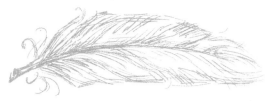

Gentleness: *I'm often not gentle with interruptions and delays, Lord, especially when I'm tired or when I'm thinking only of myself. Help me to honor You with gentle answers and responses to others, even when I'm busy or frazzled.*

Patience: *When things don't go my way, when I'm stuck in traffic or the Internet stops working at a critical moment, help me turn to You in prayer and trust instead of flailing about in anger and rage. Oh, how I need to learn patient trust in You and Your timing, knowing that You use even trials for my good and Your glory.*

Forgiveness: *How many thousands of times You have forgiven me, Father! Teach me to forgive like You do when others are not kind or humble or gentle or patient with me.*

Love: *Over and over when love is mentioned, it is given the highest place. Surely that's because without love none of these other behaviors are possible. Clothe me, Lord, with Your love, for mine is woefully insufficient.*

Peace: *Yes, Lord, may Your peace rule my unruly heart!*

Thankfulness: *How much I have to be grateful for, Lord God! Keep my eyes open to notice and recognize Your hand of blessing and guidance and grace in my life each and every day. Help me to walk in an atmosphere of thankfulness.*

What an impressive list! Every one of these virtues (yes, that's an old-fashioned word, but that's what they are) ought to distinguish the Christian. We can't force that. We can only ask God to fill us with His love—fill us to the top and overflowing. Then all these virtues will pour out of us onto others because we ourselves are so filled with His love.

This verse resonated with me: "Let the message about Christ, in all its richness, fill your lives. Teach and counsel each other with all the wisdom he gives. Sing psalms and hymns and spiritual songs to God with thankful hearts" (vs. 16).

As we close out one of my very favorite passages of Scripture, here's how I responded; feel free to pray with me:

I need to be a living message, don't I, Lord? Fill me with kindness. In our world as I write, we are experiencing a season of isolation during the COVID-19 pandemic. I cannot foresee what trial or hardship may befall us in future days, but whatever the circumstances, Lord, help me to cope and still find ways to encourage others and share the Good News in all its richness. Your gospel and the joy it brings never changes despite hard times. Father, may I truly clothe myself with all the virtues You desire. May they permeate my life and all I do. Help me to teach and sing and be thankful.

Psalm 4

For our "psalm break" we're looking at one I call a "bedtime psalm." As you read, you'll notice that the psalm progresses from David's emotional plea about troubled relationships to trust that leads to joy—and to a good night's sleep. We can learn much as we study the transformation of David's thoughts and emotions in this psalm, but that's enough from me. It's your time to dig in and see what God has to say to you from this ancient song of David.

My Reflections

Request:

Read: Psalm 4

Record:

Respond:

Anger is a strong emotion that can easily take control of our hearts and our thoughts. It rushes in upon us before we even realize it's arrived and demands instant attention. I've wrestled with anger in my own life, an emotion I feel all too easily—and often without just cause.

David begins his psalm angry. False accusations have been made against him. People are literally lying and ruining his reputation. Now it is true that David was guilty of some horrid sins in his life, but in this case, he's innocent, and having his good name smeared hurts. I ache for him when I read this psalm. Have you ever been misjudged in either action or intention? It stings. David responds with honest prayer, and that is worth noting.

I love that between each section of this psalm is a "selah" or an interlude to ponder and reflect on what has just been said or sung. Verses 1-2 comprise David's complaint.

He lays out his frustrations before God and also to the people who have wronged him. Likely they were not physically present; he's just venting his frustrations in God's presence as he prays. Yes, David starts with prayer and teaches us that no subject is off limits with God. We can always come to Him and pour out our anger, our pain, our deepest feelings. If I could just remember to pray when I'm angry, I'd be much better off.

In the next section, David reminds himself of what is true. God sets apart and cares for the godly, for those who love Him and strive to serve Him. God does answer when we call to Him. Anger itself is an emotion and not sinful until we allow our anger to control us and cause us to act in unkind or ungodly ways. Then it becomes sin. It's very helpful to remind ourselves of these truths when we're in a tizzy.

The last section of this psalm is so uplifting. We can almost feel the sigh of relief as David has now regained a "right spirit" and has chosen to trust the Lord. In fact, he's filled with greater joy than when the harvest is plentiful and safely in. And then, our David goes to sleep. Isn't that just the happiest of endings? Has his circumstance of being wronged changed? No. Has his heart settled and has his anger diminished in light of the truth that God hears and God cares? Oh, yes. Maybe I need to type this psalm out and keep it handy for easy reference when I'm upset. It's pretty much perfect for calming down a ruffled soul.

My verse today: "Don't sin by letting anger control you. Think about it overnight and remain silent. [Interlude]" (vs. 4).

I'm so personally struck by this verse. Oh, Father! Help me not to sin with harsh and unreasonable words when anger overtakes me. Instead, help me to keep silent and think about it. So often my anger is based on being thwarted in something I wanted. It's selfish and self-centered. Keep me quiet, Lord, until my spirit is quieted too. Then, let me hear from You before I speak. Thank You for this good lesson from Your Word.

Did you find a special verse that spoke to your heart? It won't be long now until you're finished with the Flight lessons and on your way, soaring without input from me, but continuing to glean wisdom from His Word with His Spirit as your guide. That's my whole goal in this devotional book—that you will soar like an eagle on powerful wings of trust and faith as you open the Bible and simply sit and meet with God without any outside helps. It's possible and it's wonderful!

(Of course, there will be times you'll want to consult a concordance or study notes for insight into perplexing passages. I'm just reminding you that as you read His words and ask for His guidance, God Himself will speak to you and give you insight.)

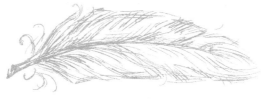

Proverbs 4

Have you ever lost your way? I remember a time when my husband had that experience on a bike trail. He missed a turn on his route and biked an additional 20 miles before he came to the next turn and realized how much farther away from the start he was than he'd calculated. His goal for that day had been around 30 miles, but he ended up biking over 50 miles. Poor guy. He soaked in the tub a long time that night.

Today, we're pondering choices. King Solomon has a lot to say about the right path to take and the wrong one. In this case, though, choosing the wrong path is much more damaging than a few extra miles on a bike trail. May we read and gain wisdom.

My Reflections

Request:

Read: Proverbs 4

Record:

Respond:

Sharon's notes:

Proverbs is often a challenge for me. I have a hard time choosing just one verse, because almost every verse touches my soul and teaches me. The verse that impressed me today: "The way of the righteous is like the first gleam of dawn, which shines ever brighter until the full light of day" (vs. 18). *I love this thought, Lord. The more we walk with You on the right path, the clearer and brighter the way becomes. This is how You work in our lives when we walk in Your way. And the opposite is also true. Straying from Your path results in fuzzy confusion, an inability to see You clearly. Thank You for this beautiful, instructive verse.*

Several other great verses in this passage also caught my attention, and because I have the privilege of writing to you, I'm grateful we can explore them as well. One of the overarching themes of Proverbs—and of this beginning section in particular—is the theme of listening to good advice. I totally understand Solomon's pleading. I remember over the years pleading with friends to make wise choices, knowing full well how cataclysmic bad choices could be for them.

When you love someone, you want the best for him or her. You long for them to have a life filled with blessing, peace, hope, and the right kind of adventures. No one wants their loved ones to walk away from all that will bring lasting happiness. Solomon's writing here is forceful and direct: ". . . listen when your father corrects you . . ." (vs. 1b). ". . . Don't forget my words or turn away from them" (vs. 5b). "Don't turn your back on wisdom . . ." (vs. 6a). "Take hold of my instructions; don't let them go. Guard them . . ." (vs. 13a). These proverbs are not just interesting ideas that one might choose or discard. Making good life decisions can literally mean the difference between life and death.

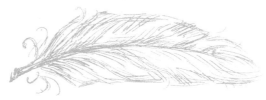

I was pondering how this works. Imagine with me a lonely Christian girl trying to gain footing in a new town. Perhaps she's just starting out in a new career. Her co-workers are friendly, but are clearly not choosing Christ-focused lives. They invite her to dabble in recreational drugs and urge her to loosen up her moral standards. What does she do? If she refuses to hang out with them after work, she fears they will shun her. The thought of that empty apartment is bleak. She has a choice to make.

One choice is to visit local churches and seek out friendships there. This can be discouraging at times and takes perseverance, especially if the first church or two seem unwilling to welcome her. However, if our imaginary girl chooses to risk more temporary loneliness and search for Christian friendships, she will eventually find herself on that good path, learning truths that stand the test of time, and finding deep friendships that last. She will not struggle, perhaps for a lifetime, with the regrets of waking up in strangers' beds or overdosing on what she thought would be mild.

The easier choice—at least at first—is to go along with the crowd "just a bit." Proverbs 4:15 warns: "Don't even think about it; don't go that way. Turn away and keep moving." Stay too long in situations where you are the only one with your values, and you'll find either mocking from those who are irritated you're not joining in or you'll find that slowly your language becomes more coarse and your choices to indulge in wrong kinds of activities become more frequent. And then the guilt of it all reinforces the behavior as you think to yourself (falsely) that it's too late now. I've watched this play out way too many times.

Does this mean our girl cannot be friendly and kind to her co-workers? Of course not. Does she need to get all judgy on them? No. But she does need to guard her heart: "Guard your heart above all else, for it determines the course of your life" (vs. 23). She does need to seek out people who will help her maintain her desire to serve God and walk in His paths. Oh, how we need each other as Christians!

> Look straight ahead, and fix your eyes on what lies before you.
> Mark out a straight path for your feet; stay on the safe path.
> Don't get sidetracked; keep your feet from following evil.
> —Proverbs 4:25-27

P.S. If you are that girl who walked a little way or a long way down the wrong path, do not listen to the lies that you can't turn around. Review all we learned in the Nest. When you ask God to forgive you, He forgives. He sees you as spotless and clean because of Jesus' sacrifice. Receive His forgiveness and revel that you are His fully loved, fully clean, fully forgiven daughter. He's longing for your return, and it's never too late.

Colossians 3:18-4:1

If you work for someone else, how are you doing as an employee? If you're married, how is it going with your spouse? Today's lesson is a highly practical guide from Paul on how to live and work with others successfully. I'm so very thankful that slavery is not legal these days. Sometimes, however, working for a difficult employer can feel like a kind of slavery, especially if for some reason you feel trapped in your job. May God grant you eyes to see His lessons for you in this passage of Scripture as you read.

My Reflections

Request:

Read: Colossians 3:18-4:1

Record:

Respond:

Sharon's notes:

I was impressed by the advice Paul gave the Colossians all about daily living with others in harmony and love. Here are the lessons I gleaned that I hope will bless you as well.

Submission is a beautiful way to put others ahead of our own selfish selves. All Christians are required to be willing to lay aside our desires for the good of others. Jesus is our greatest example. "Though he was God, he did not think of equality with God as something to cling to. Instead, he gave up his divine privileges; he took the humble position of a slave . . ." (Philippians 2:6-7a).

True sacrificial love is required of all Christians. Paul spells out what love looks like to those who are considered authorities. Love is never harsh. Never. That's a telling statement to husbands and masters in a day when their society granted almost limitless freedom to treat those under their care in any way they chose. Even in the parenting role, fathers in particular are warned not to aggravate their kids. How cool is that? Paul clearly gives the reason: We are not to discourage those we love—and harsh and demanding behavior is definitely discouraging.

Obedience and work are ultimately done to honor God. Whether or not our employer or master or parent or spouse is watching, we are to complete tasks honorably and thoroughly. God always watches, and He is pleased when we do our best at tasks without laziness or spite.

Those in authority are also watched by God, and He expects fairness from those who have responsibility over the lives of others. You see, in God's Kingdom we are all equal before Him and equally responsible to live out submission, love, and obedience with integrity. No one has the right to lord it over anyone else. Jesus stated that very firmly:

> But Jesus called them together and said, "You know that the rulers in this world lord it over their people, and officials flaunt their authority over those under them. But among you it will be different. Whoever wants to be a leader among you must be your servant, and whoever wants to be first among you must become your slave. For even the Son of Man came not to be served but to serve others and to give his life as a ransom for many." —Matthew 20:25-28

As we close, I share my verse with you. "Husbands, love your wives and never treat them harshly" (Colossians 3:19). I was so struck by the way God defines what a husband's love should look like.

Lord God, when You talk about people in charge, You always flip it. You did not come to be served but to serve, Lord Jesus. And here You tell husbands who are in charge to love and to never be harsh. Leadership under Your command looks a whole lot like loving servanthood. Thank You for this teaching.

We've had much to reflect on in today's passage. I've been challenged anew to walk in submission and servant-hearted love in my dealings with others. Also, I want to keep in mind that whatever I do, I do it for the God who sees and loves me.

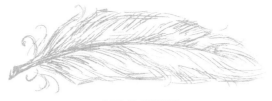

Colossians 4:2-18

We talked a lot about servant leadership yesterday. Today, I was reminded in our passage that Paul was in prison when he wrote Colossians. Yes. I had to be reminded. Paul has not mentioned his chains and his difficult circumstances in his letter at all. His teaching has been all about Jesus and following Him with all our hearts. He has focused on the Colossians and good instruction for them. What a great example he is. As you read, you'll see that as Paul closes out his letter, we're given a strong glimpse of his personality and his current position in prison.

My Reflections

Request:

Read: Colossians 4:2-18

Record:

Respond:

Sharon's notes:

As I read this last portion of Paul's letter, I found three themes: prison, people, and prayer. Ponder them with me as we close out this remarkable book of the Bible.

First, as I mentioned, I was made aware again that Paul was in prison when he wrote this letter. I love how Paul viewed his imprisonment. He shares with us in verse 3 that he's in chains for a purpose—opportunities to serve God. Yes, even there. What a truth for us to absorb! Wherever we find ourselves, if God has allowed us to be in that place at that time, He has a purpose in it. That changes the way I view hard times. Instead of sitting in a pity puddle and splashing mud all over myself, I can walk through that puddle looking for the opportunities God has for me to honor Him right where I am. Paul did that so well from prison. His only other mention of his confinement is to be grateful for the people who visit and bring him comfort. We have to really stop and remember how difficult imprisonment must have been in those days. Paul certainly doesn't complain

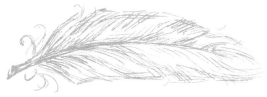

about it or tell us any harrowing details. All we read about is gratitude for comfort and contentment in serving. This humbles me greatly, since that is often not my attitude in far less grave situations.

Second, I love Paul's emphasis on individual people. He doesn't just give theological lectures to the masses. It's a real letter, and he sends greetings to and from real people. He interacts with and deeply loves these individuals. Here are the names he mentions just so you can marvel with me at the sheer number of them: Timothy, Tychicus, Onesimus, Aristarchus, Mark, Barnabas, Justus, Epaphras, Luke, Demas, Nympha, and Archippus. Paul loved these dear people. He refers to them as brothers, beloved, co-workers, faithful, bringing comfort, and earnestly prayerful. Paul notices people. He's quick to praise them and encourage them. He's free with his gratitude and blessing. I want to be like Paul.

Third, Paul also emphasizes the importance of prayer in this last portion of Colossians. Our section opened with his command to "Devote yourselves to prayer with an alert mind and a thankful heart" (Colossians 4:2). The word "devote" tells us that prayer is of the utmost importance. Google dictionary defines "devote" this way: "(to) give all or a large part of one's time or resources to (a person, activity, or cause)." Prayer is a big deal. Paul believes he will be more successful in sharing Christ if the Colossians pray, inviting God's intervention and presence in his work. Prayer matters. Paul commends Epaphras because "he always prays earnestly for you, asking God to make you strong and perfect, fully confident that you are following the whole will of God" (Colossians 4:12b). What a wonderful prayer!

Colossians 4:2 was my verse today because of that word "devote," and here's my response: *Paul is talking about serious prayer here. Not just a recited creed or a set of words so memorized that one no longer engages the mind while repeating them. These words are strong. "Be devoted." Lord, help me. Help me to be devoted, dedicated, passionate, and purposeful about prayer. "With an alert mind." Father, help me to be wide awake as I intercede, open to hearing the Spirit who helps me pray. "And a thankful heart." Help me to always come to You fully and humbly aware of every good gift You have given me.*

I love Epaphras' prayer so dearly and use it as my prayer for you: *Father God, will You please make the readers of this book strong and perfect, fully confident that they are following Your whole will. Help them to grow because they are feeding on Your living Word given to nourish and strengthen. Help me, as well, Lord to rely on You and Your words as I attempt to live out Your whole will in my life. Help us all to yield, Lord Jesus. We yield. In Your mighty Name and for Your great glory, Amen.*

Philemon 1-10

Today and tomorrow we'll focus on one of the many people Paul mentioned in his letter to the Colossians, Onesimus, one of our main characters today. He writes: "I am also sending Onesimus, a faithful and beloved brother, one of your own people. He and Tychicus will tell you everything that's happening here" (Colossians 4:9). I just love the way Paul describes Onesimus as a "faithful and beloved brother." He was also a runaway slave. He had fled from a Christian convert in Colossae named Philemon, and it's possible that he had even stolen from Philemon as he ran. The punishment for runaway slaves was severe and could have resulted in death. Instead, God orchestrated events so that Onesimus met Paul in Rome and received Christ as his Savior. How astounding is that! Onesimus is now returning to his former master, Philemon. He carries with him a letter from Paul to Philemon, once his master and now his brother in Christ. It's a phenomenal letter of grace and petition and teaching. As you study the first portion of the letter today, may God show you wonderful lessons from His Word.

My Reflections

Request:

Read: Philemon 1-10

Record:

Respond:

Sharon's notes:

I love the way Paul refers to Philemon—not that different from his description of Onesimus in Colossians. He calls Philemon a "beloved co-worker." As Paul writes to Philemon, he comes from a strong position of love for both men, the master and the slave. In Christ, of course, they are equals, sinners saved by grace and equipped with the Holy Spirit's gifts to share the gospel with others. Isn't that the way we should all interact with other believers? Each one is a beloved of God and of ours because they are part of the family.

Note how Paul praises Philemon for his kindness and his growth as a Christian. Paul doesn't start with his request. First, he establishes his deep love for Philemon. I don't know about you (although I have a strong hunch), but I can definitely receive

hard words better from people I know are for me. When I'm secure in their love and their desire for my best, then I can hear what they have to share without defensiveness or anger. This is how we tackle tough things with others. We start with . . . *beloved*.

Let's step back for a minute, though, and think about this tiny little one-chapter book in the Bible. It was written on behalf of a slave! The entire book is dedicated to the happiness and well-being of one who would have been pretty near the bottom of the barrel in terms of prestige in that day and age. God wants us to know that no one is insignificant to Him. We also see a wonderful lesson here on the value God places on all human beings, no matter their current state as slave or free, rich or poor.

Although this letter is directed toward Philemon, we should note that his church family is also addressed. "This letter is from Paul, a prisoner for preaching the Good News about Christ Jesus, and from our brother Timothy. I am writing to Philemon, our beloved co-worker, and to our sister Apphia, and to our fellow soldier Archippus, and to the church that meets in your house" (Philemon 1-2). So this is not just a note to one man; it's a "family affair." The church is involved because now that Onesimus is a believer, he has equal standing in the church with Philemon. Each brother in Christ must treat the other with love and respect. When we join a church body, we become family with each other and can and should be held accountable for the way we treat one another. That's a huge blessing of belonging to a local church body. People care about us and want God's best for us. (Even if Onesimus had not been a Christian, God still tells us to love. Even then. We don't get a "pass" in our behavior toward one who doesn't know God. But that's a discussion for another time.)

I was fascinated by the way Paul presented his request and the purpose of his letter. I chose this as my passage to ponder: "That is why I am boldly asking a favor of you. I could demand it in the name of Christ because it is the right thing for you to do. But because of our love, I prefer simply to ask you . . ." (Philemon 8-9a). Then I talked to the Lord as I thought about that verse.

Paul doesn't bully Philemon into forgiving and doing what is right. He comes as a humble petitioner and asks. This is the way of grace. Lord, forgive me when I'm harsh and hard and demanding. Help me to win people to right ways of thinking by love and gentleness instead. Thank You for this example. Thank You that Paul gave Philemon the dignity of personal choice to do what was right. So much like You, Father God, who pleads with His obstinate creation to turn and be saved.

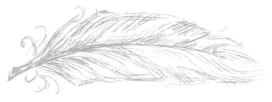

Philemon 11-25

I have this curiosity issue when I read the Bible. I love reading all the stories, but I end up with so many questions. I always want to know more, want more backstory! Like . . . why did Onesimus run away? Was Philemon a kind master? How did Onesimus end up meeting Paul? Was he in prison briefly or did other Christians find him and help him or did he seek out Paul due to feeling guilt for running? How long had Onesimus been gone? What did it look like when this runaway slave realized he could be free in Christ? How I love that each person on this planet has an amazing story all their own. How I love that God sees and knows each of us and calls us—"come to Me."

My Reflections

Request:

Read: Philemon 11-25

Record:

Respond:

We learn a bit more about our runaway slave from this second section of Paul's letter to Philemon. We learn that the name Onesimus actually means "useful," and he has been useful to Paul. Evidently, he hadn't lived up to his name when he worked for Philemon, but was now a changed man. In fact, he had become more than useful to Paul; he had become like a son—and it is with great reluctance that Paul parts with him.

We also see a hint in this passage that Onesimus may have stolen money or items from Philemon's home. I love that Paul doesn't ask Philemon to forgive the theft, although he certainly could have. Instead, Paul offers to pay any debts owed to Philemon. His request of leniency for Onesimus comes with the full knowledge that Philemon has lost a laborer who will need to be replaced and that he may have lost even more. Paul is willing to give of his own money to make this right.

And Paul longs to keep Onesimus! Paul isn't asking to buy him. In fact, Paul encourages those who are slaves to acquire their freedom legally if they can. "Are you a slave? Don't let that worry you—but if you get a chance to be free, take it. And remember, if you were a slave when the Lord called you, you are now free in the Lord. And if you were free when the Lord called you, you are now a slave of Christ" (1 Corinthians 7:21-22). Paul views Onesimus as a beloved brother who would be useful to him in his work. How honored Onesimus must have felt to be esteemed in this way. How humbling to know that Paul is prepared to personally pay any debts and cover any wrongs. What a beautiful redemption story! Onesimus is redeemed from death and sin by Christ's saving grace, and he is redeemed from his debt to Philemon by Paul's loving generosity. Paul doesn't just talk about grace and giving. Paul models it for us, as a leader who follows Christ should.

We see again in this section Paul's respect for Philemon. "I wanted to keep him here with me while I am in these chains for preaching the Good News, and he would have helped me on your behalf. But I didn't want to do anything without your consent. I wanted you to help because you were willing, not because you were forced" (Philemon 13-14). Paul managed to show grace and respect for both men in an amazingly diplomatic way. Reading this letter to Philemon has been very helpful in teaching me how to deal with difficult situations between brothers and sisters in Christ. Paul's loving, hands-on approach is fantastic.

As we finish up our study of Philemon, I share "my" verse with you. "He is no longer like a slave to you. He is more than a slave, for he is a beloved brother, especially to me. Now he will mean much more to you, both as a man and as a brother in the Lord" (vs. 16). As I pondered Paul's words about Onesimus, here was my response to the Lord.

I love the way Paul speaks of Onesimus, Father. He is not "less than" or considered mere property in any way. Instead, Paul sees him as a beloved brother and fellow man. He's every bit as significant as anyone else on the planet—and he's "family" now that he has received Christ. Thank You, God, that You are no respecter of persons. We are all under You and of great value because You loved us enough to redeem us, purchasing us back with Your own precious blood.

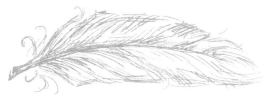

Psalm 5

Before we leave this section of our book, Flight, to begin the last section, Soar, we'll look at one more psalm and proverb together. Today, we study Psalm 5 that begins with a morning prayer. Verse 3 summarizes the prayer with this petition: "Listen to my voice in the morning, LORD. Each morning I bring my requests to you and wait expectantly."

I wonder when you take your set-apart time with God. For most people, mornings are best before the busyness and bustle of the day take us farther and farther away from a quiet space to be alone with Him. Whether your time is morning or not, it's a wonderful practice to start each day with prayer. May we be like David and bring our requests each morning, waiting expectantly for His answers.

My Reflections

Request:

Read: Psalm 5

Record:

Respond:

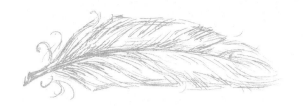

I'm always struck by the great number of psalms that appeal to God about enemies. As king—and even before he became king—David simply had a lot of enemies. He fought Goliath; he fled from Saul; he was continually challenged by the nations bordering Israel. Quite naturally as he brought his troubles before the Lord, his prayers included enemy troubles. In our lives, we may not battle adversaries that are physically attacking us.

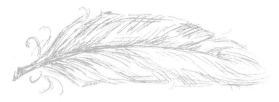

Our enemies may be relationship struggles or hurt feelings, depression or anger or envy. Or possibly we do genuinely have people in our lives that hate us and wish us harm. Whatever troubles us is an enemy of our souls, and we can bring it to God honestly and completely. With David, it was often physical enemies, but what comfort and relief I feel when I bring my "enemies" to the Lord, present them honestly before God in prayer, and seek His help. How thankful I am for David's example, that his prayer life includes all of life—his great joys and his great distresses.

My favorite part of this psalm is the ending. It reflects our ministry verse at Sweet Selah Ministries: "He will cover you with his feathers. He will shelter you with his wings. His faithful promises are your armor and protection" (Psalm 91:4). The whole imagery of being protected and sheltered securely under great and marvelous wings is one that blesses and comforts me. David must feel the same way, because he often alludes to God's covering and protection. Here is what he writes in our psalm, "But let all who take refuge in you rejoice; let them sing joyful praises forever. Spread your protection over them, that all who love your name may be filled with joy. For you bless the godly, O Lord; you surround them with your shield of love" (vs. 11-12).

Those beautiful words fill me with comfort. That's why I love reading God's Word every single day. I need to be reminded often of His love for me. When I walk out into the day assured and happy that my God cares, that He is with me, I can face any troubles with calm and peace. Here are a few of the ways God says "I love you" in these two last verses of the psalm:

He is a refuge for us.
He brings rejoicing and fills our hearts with singing.
He spreads His protection over us.
He fills us with joy.
He blesses us, His children.
He surrounds us with His "shield of love."
— Psalm 5:11-12 (paraphrased)

These are the verses I chose as "mine"—and knowing His love and knowing He is with me, I'm set to have a wonderful day.

Dear Father, I love the thought of You spreading protection over me. Like great big wings over a tiny bird or a warm quilt enfolding me. To know that You cover me brings immense joy. You fill me with Your joy. All who are protected by Your loving cover break out in joyful praise! I love being Yours. Amen.

Proverbs 5

In this chapter Solomon strongly warns his sons about the dangers of sexual immorality and implores them to stay faithful to their wives, not straying from the marriage bed. He talks about the horrific consequences of heartbreak and ruin for those who refuse to heed. You might wonder what this passage says to women since it was written to sons. As always, God has much to say in every part of His Word, so I ask you to read our chapter carefully, asking God for His wisdom. Then, let's talk after you have selected a verse and responded to the Lord yourself. When we request His help . . . He shows us His heart. Every chapter in the Bible is for all God's people—men and women alike—and filled with much to learn. Read on, be warned, and be blessed.

My Reflections

Request:

Read: Proverbs 5

Record:

Respond:

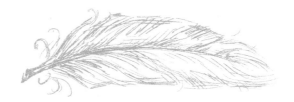

Sharon's notes:

I was struck by the urgent tone of Solomon's warnings to his sons in this passage. He acknowledged that sexual sin looks alluring and pleasant and downright fun at first. However, he tells his sons and all who read his proverbs that giving way to temptation to evil ends in disaster. And herein lie the truth and the heart of the matter.

God's rules on marriage and sexual fidelity, on self-control and faithfulness are very clear. We are only to enjoy marital pleasures . . . in marriage. That's the bottom line. He made us. He knows what will ultimately satisfy us without a sting. When we walk away from His wisdom in this or in any area of temptation, we walk into ruin and disaster.

Notice some of the words Solomon uses to make his point. "But in the end she is as bitter as poison, as dangerous as a double-edged sword. Her feet go down to death; her steps lead straight to the grave" (vs. 4-5). This is where sin leads. Especially, this is where

sexual sin leads. In every culture, in every time, and in every place throughout history, we find the temptation to abuse sexuality. God gave us a powerfully beautiful way to unite as one flesh with our spouse, symbolizing a union that is profoundly more than physical. Sadly, men and women have decided to extract the pleasure and reproduce it outside the confines and safety of a marriage covenant—to their own ultimate detriment and despair. Without a lifelong commitment, the vulnerability of a sexual relationship shames and strips and destroys. God created us for marriages of commitment and fidelity.

What can I learn from this? I can learn to guard my heart and my body from anyone who is not my husband. I can celebrate sexual love within the safety of the marriage covenant. And, if I'm single, I can keep myself apart from anything that would ultimately harm my body and poison me. These strong words need to be heeded.

What if you have not kept your body for marriage? What then? Oh, this is where the grace of God is so marvelously apparent. He forgives all our sins and hurls them into the depths of the sea. And He washes us clean. "'Come now, let's settle this,' says the LORD. 'Though your sins are like scarlet, I will make them as white as snow. Though they are red like crimson, I will make them as white as wool'" (Isaiah 1:18). Don't cringe and hide and run from God when you've sinned. Rather, go to Him knowing that in His grace and in His gentleness He is longing to forgive you and restore you. Then commit yourself to purity. He will help you. And if you fall again? He will be there to help again. Our God is filled with kindness and goodness to us without measure.

The verse that stood out to me in this chapter was: "An evil man is held captive by his own sins; they are ropes that catch and hold him" (vs. 22). I see such truth in this. Sin holds us captive. Thank God for Jesus who came to set captives free!

Lord, the heartrending truth in this verse grieves me and teaches me. When we think we need no rules . . . when we decide to satisfy every craving . . . we end up as captives— tied down by the very things that enticed us. Help me, Lord, to guard my choices wisely all my life. How I thank You that because of Christ I am no longer a slave to sin! Glory Hallelujah! Amen.

How I have loved studying God's Word with you! He has led us through some quite diverse places. His Word is wonderfully rich and varied and full. He meets every need and helps with every question as we consistently meet with Him and soak in the truths found in this love letter written to you and me. I hope, as you look back on your notes, you see with wonder and awe all that God has taught you as you have come to Him with eagerness to learn. And more adventure awaits. Turn the page tomorrow and prepare to soar!

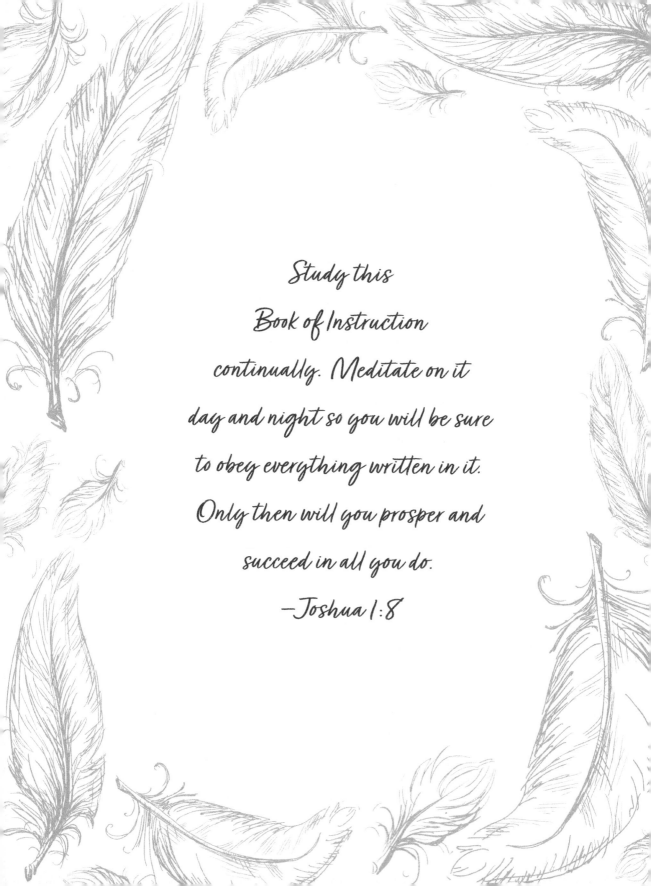

Study this
Book of Instruction
continually. Meditate on it
day and night so you will be sure
to obey everything written in it.
Only then will you prosper and
succeed in all you do.

—Joshua 1:8

Soar

Soar Introduction

Study this Book of Instruction continually. Meditate on it day and
night so you will be sure to obey everything written in it. Only then
will you prosper and succeed in all you do. —Joshua 1:8

• • • • • • • • • • • • • • • • • • •

Here we are. We've traveled for a couple of months now studying God's Word together. I've loved this journey and have imagined you all along the way, growing in your faith and your ability to steadily meet with God for this set-apart time each day. I'm very proud of you. Your desire to study His Word and to know Him better—and to make it this far—is praiseworthy. I know you've relied on God's strength to do this. We need Him and His Spirit to give us the self-control to choose quiet times each day. I suspect you had days and maybe even weeks when you dropped by the wayside, and that's okay too. Every time you started up again, the habit of a daily time with God and His Word was embedded more deeply into your brain and into the rhythm of your life. And here you are today ready to journey on alone. Good job. Hooray! Well done.

As you begin this last section of the book—and perhaps then turn to our companion book, *Give Me Wings to Soar Journal*—you will choose the book in God's Word you want to study. If you wish you can pick a Bible reading plan. Many good ones are available, and I've listed some suggestions for you on page 250. Whatever you choose, I'm praying that you will not give up. Use the blank journal pages in this section to continue your daily deep dive into God's Word, *requesting* His help, *reading* a short passage thoroughly, *recording* a verse, and *responding* to the Lord from your heart.

When Joshua found himself in command after the death of Moses, I think he must have been quite apprehensive. Moses had led the Israelites out of Egypt and through the desert for forty years, listening to God and following His commands along the way. Phenomenal miracles had been seen as God rescued His people. And now Joshua's beloved mentor was gone, and it was up to him to hear from God and lead God's people in step with His instructions. In Joshua 1, we find Joshua listening. In fact, the first ten

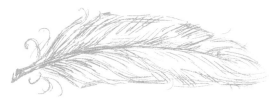

verses in my Bible are titled, "The Lord's Charge to Joshua." These lines from verse 1 are a part of that charge—and are written to us as well:

Study this Book of Instruction continually. Commands like this one are the reason we choose to meet daily with God in His Word. We need to hear from Him continually.

Meditate on it day and night so you will be sure to obey everything written in it. We don't just read the Bible, we write out verses, we write our responses. We let the words and the meaning sink deep into our hearts and minds by meditating on them. It is through this kind of study that we learn God's commands—and we have to know them to obey them.

Only then will you prosper and succeed in all you do. To prosper and succeed as a follower of Christ we need to be in His Word, studying and meditating and obeying.

How thankful I am that you have journeyed with me from Nest to Flight! I hope and pray that from now until the day Jesus calls you home to Heaven you will meet with Him through His living Word and prayer each day. That is truly the path to abundant life.

Now, dear reader, you've nested and know where to go for rest. You've learned to fly and study God's Word devotionally. Stretch those beautiful wings of yours, lean hard on the Holy Spirit who guides and holds you . . . *and Soar!*

Reading Ideas

You may already have a wonderful reading plan to follow for your first solo soaring flight. But in case you want some ideas, I'm including them on the next page. Whatever you choose, continue the pattern of reading no more than a chapter a day and far less than a chapter if you wish. Read short passages and study them deeply using the 4R Method.

If you like the journaling pages you find here in the Soar section, consider purchasing our *Give Me Wings to Soar Journal*. Its pages look like the ones here in this section, and an overview of the 4R Method is included to encourage you. Of course, you don't need the journal, but it's available, and I think you'll enjoy it and find it helpful.

I'd love to hear from you, what plan you choose and what God has taught you. Please feel free to write me at sharon@sweetselah.org, and if you wish to be extra generous with your time, reviews on Amazon and other booksellers' sites are always appreciated to help others find this book.

Love and thanks,

Sharon

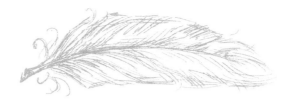

❧ Read one of the four gospels and learn more about Jesus' life.

❧ Alternate between an Old Testament book and a New Testament book.

❧ Using a chronological Bible, take your time and follow the Bible story from beginning to end. Expect it to take 5-7 years if you are carefully using the 4R Method.

❧ Study the book of Acts and learn more about Paul, who wrote Colossians and Philemon.

❧ Choose a read-through Bible plan from a reliable source, but instead of doing the plan in a year, use it as a guide for five years or more.

❧ Find a friend and start a Give Me Wings to Soar Bible study. Choose a book of the Bible and divide it into readings for a week at a time. Request, Read, Record, and Respond in your Soar journal, then meet each week to discuss and share what each of you has gleaned.

❧ Expand to a church-wide Bible study and choose a book or books to study, then meet in small groups once a week, sharing the insights God has given you.

❧ Follow your pastor's sermons by studying the book of the Bible he's currently using for messages on Sunday mornings.

❧ Be text pals or email pals with a friend at a distance, daily sharing your verse and your response

The book of the Bible I've chosen to read next is:

Turn the page and begin your first day to soar!

DAY 64 SOAR

My Reflections

Request

Read

Record

Respond

My Reflections

Request

Read

Record

Respond

My Reflections

Request

Read

Record

Respond

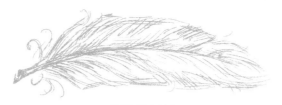

My Reflections

Request

Read

Record

Respond

My Reflections

Request

Read

Record

Respond

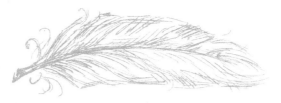

My Reflections

Request

Read

Record

Respond

DAY 70 SOAR

My Reflections

Request

Read

Record

Respond

My Reflections

Request

Read

Record

Respond

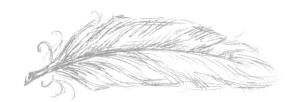

My Reflections

Request

Read

Record

Respond

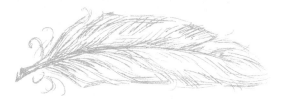

DAY 73 SOAR

My Reflections

Request

Read

Record

Respond

My Reflections

Request

Read

Record

Respond

My Reflections

Request

Read

Record

Respond

Meet the Author, Sharon Gamble

Hello, Dear Reader!

I wish we could get to know each other over a cup of tea, my favorite way to "meet" someone! Since that's unlikely, here's a bit about me and who I am.

I love people and excitement and parties. Especially tea parties with a few close friends. I also love quiet and creating space to be still with God. In fact, I've grown to love that most of all.

I think nearly all of us know very well without any help how to be busy. But fitting in intentional time to meet with God? That can be tricky. Sharing with women ways to find that time, to know Him more intimately, and grow to love Him more deeply is my passion and my happiness and my sweet spot for sure.

Throughout my life journey, I've collected quotes that have touched me and found Bible verses that have sustained me. I've learned truths that have shaped me. All that God is teaching me in the everyday stories of life, I'm thrilled to pass on to you with a grateful heart.

In fact, God stirred me to form Sweet Selah Ministries that I might share through writing and speaking the insight and thoughts and lessons He is teaching me.

My husband and I live in beautiful New Hampshire with our little "teddy bear pup," Bella Grace. We belong to a great church and love hanging out with our home group every other Friday night.

In the summer, we can often be found bicycling. We have a ton of winding, quaint back roads around here, and our bikes know them all. In the winter, we tromp in the snow and build fires in our fireplace and sip hot chocolate.

We are parents to two wonderful daughters and their dearly-loved husbands, and we are Nina and Papa to an ever-growing bunch of the sweetest grandkids ever.

Along the way, through the ups and downs have come life lessons:

- ✤ I've failed and learned that failure isn't fatal.
- ✤ I've overachieved myself into basket-case status.
- ✤ I've stumbled to God in a mess and felt His arms hold me close.
- ✤ I've seen the hand of God move in miraculous ways, over and over again.
- ✤ I'm still on the journey of knowing Him better and loving Him more.

I'd love to stay connected with you. Write me anytime at sharon@sweetselah.org and sign up for my blog, Monday Musings. You can check it out at sweetselah.org.

You are loved,

Sharon

Made in the USA
Middletown, DE
27 November 2020